KASPAR AND OTHER PLAYS

KASPAR

AND OTHER PLAYS

BY PETER HANDKE

TRANSLATED BY MICHAEL ROLOFF

HILL AND WANG

A division of Farrar, Straus and Giroux

New York

ISBN 0-809-01546-3
Printed in the United States of America
Library of Congress catalog card number: 78–103704
Designed by Kay Rexrode

First published in 1969 by Farrar, Straus and Giroux
This edition first published in 1989 by Hill and Wang
Nineteenth printing, 2000

CONTENTS

A NOTE ON THE TRANSLATION

In translating the invective at the end of *Offending the Audience*, I translated the principle according to which they are arranged—that is, I sought to create new acoustic patterns in English—rather than translate each epithet literally, which would only have resulted in completely discordant patterns.

To the assortment of moral truisms of which the prompters have a choice when they address Kaspar, I have added a number of American platitudes; the imaginative reader will have no difficulty in supplying even more. Certain liberties have also been taken to make Kaspar's rhymes sort of rhyme. In nearly every other respect, these are translations and not adaptations. Peter Handke himself has cut the last sentence in *Self-Accusation* and also Kaspar's final sentence which appeared in the original version.

M.R.

NOTE ON OFFENDING THE AUDIENCE
AND SELF-ACCUSATION

The speak-ins (*Sprechstücke*) are spectacles without pictures, inasmuch as they give no picture of the world. They point to the world not by way of pictures but by way of words; the words of the speak-ins don't point at the world as something lying outside the words but to the world in the words themselves. The words that make up the speak-ins give no picture of the world but a concept of it. The speak-ins are theatrical inasmuch as they employ natural forms of expression found in reality. They employ only such expressions as are natural in real speech; that is, they employ the speech forms that are uttered *orally* in real life. The speak-ins employ natural examples of swearing, of self-indictment, of confession, of testimony, of interrogation, of justification, of evasion, of prophecy, of calls for help. Therefore they need a vis-à-vis, at least *one* person who listens; otherwise, they would not be natural but extorted by the author. It is to that extent that my speak-ins are pieces for the theater. Ironically, they imitate the gestures of all the given devices natural to the theater.

The speak-ins have no action, since every action on stage would only be the picture of another action. The speak-ins confine themselves, by obeying their natural form, to words. They give no pictures, not even pictures in word form, which would only be pictures the author extorted to represent an internal, unexpressed, wordless circumstance and not a *natural* expression.

Speak-ins are autonomous prologues to the old plays. They do not want to revolutionize, but to make aware.

Peter Handke

OFFENDING THE AUDIENCE

*for Karlheinz Braun, Claus Peymann, Basch
Peymann, Wolfgang Wiens, Peter Steinbach,
Michael Gruner, Ulrich Hass, Claus Dieter Reents,
Rüdiger Vogler, John Lennon*

CAST: FOUR SPEAKERS

Rules for the actors

Listen to the litanies in the Catholic churches.
Listen to football teams being cheered on and booed.
Listen to the rhythmic chanting at demonstrations.
Listen to the wheels of a bicycle upturned on its seat spinning until the spokes have come to rest and watch the spokes until they have reached their resting point.
Listen to the gradually increasing noise a concrete mixer makes after the motor has been started.
Listen to debaters cutting each other off.
Listen to "Tell Me" by the Rolling Stones.
Listen to the simultaneous arrival and departure of trains.
Listen to the hit parade on Radio Luxembourg.
Listen in on the simultaneous interpreters at the United Nations.
Listen to the dialogue between the gangster (Lee J. Cobb) and the pretty girl in "The Trap," when the girl asks the gangster how many more people he intends to kill; whereupon the gangster asks, as he leans back, How many are left? and watch the gangster as he says it.
See the Beatles' movies.
In "A Hard Day's Night" watch Ringo's smile at the moment when, after having been teased by the others, he sits down at his drums and begins to play.
Watch Gary Cooper's face in "The Man From the West." In the same movie watch the death of the mute as he runs down the deserted street of the lifeless town with a bullet in him, hopping and jumping and emitting those shrill screams.
Watch monkeys aping people and llamas spitting in the zoo.
Watch the behavior of bums and idlers as they amble on the street and play the machines in the penny arcades.

When the theatergoers enter the room into which they are meant to go, they are greeted by the usual pre-performance atmosphere. One might let them hear noises from behind the curtain, noises that make believe that scenery is being shifted about. For example, a table is dragged across the stage, or several chairs are noisily set up and then removed. One might let the spectators in the first few rows hear directions whispered by make-believe stage managers and the whispered interchanges between make-believe stagehands behind the curtain. Or, even better, use tape recordings of other performances in which, before the curtain rises, objects are really shifted about. These noises should be amplified to make them more audible, and perhaps should be stylized and arranged so as to produce their own order and uniformity.

The usual theater atmosphere should prevail. The ushers should be more assiduous than usual, even more formal and ceremonious, should subdue their usual whispering with even more style, so that their behavior becomes infectious. The programs should be elegant. The buzzer signals should not be forgotten; the signals are repeated at successively briefer intervals. The gradual dimming of the lights should be even more gradual if possible; perhaps the lights can be dimmed in successive stages. As the ushers proceed to close the doors, their gestures should become particularly solemn and noticeable. Yet, they are only ushers. Their actions should not appear symbolic. Late-comers should not be admitted. Inappropriately dressed ticket holders should not be admitted. The concept of what is sartorially inappropriate should be strictly applied. None of the spectators should call attention to himself or offend the eye by his attire. The men should be dressed in dark jackets, with white shirts and inconspicuous ties. The women should shun bright colors.

There is no standing-room. Once the doors are closed and the lights dim, it gradually becomes quiet behind the curtain too. The silence

OFFENDING THE AUDIENCE

behind the curtain and the silence in the auditorium are alike. The spectators stare a while longer at the almost imperceptibly fluttering curtain, which may perhaps billow once or twice as though someone had hurriedly crossed the stage. Then the curtain grows still. There is a short pause. The curtain slowly parts, allowing an unobstructed view. Once the stage is completely open to view, the four speakers step forward from upstage. Nothing impedes their progress. The stage is empty. As they walk forward noncommittally, dressed casually, it becomes light on stage as well as in the audience. The light on stage and in the auditorium is of the same intensity as at the end of a performance and there is no glare to hurt the eyes. The stage and the auditorium remain lighted throughout the performance. Even as they approach, the speakers don't look at the audience. They don't direct the words they are speaking at the audience. Under no circumstance should the audience get the impression that the words are directed at them. As far as the speakers are concerned, the audience does not yet exist. As they approach, they move their lips. Gradually their words become intelligible and finally they become loud. The invectives they deliver overlap one another. The speakers speak pell-mell. They pick up each other's words. They take words out of each other's mouths. They speak in unison, each uttering different words. They repeat. They grow louder. They scream. They pass rehearsed words from mouth to mouth. Finally, they rehearse one word in unison. The words they use in this prologue are the following (their order is immaterial): *You chuckleheads, you small-timers, you nervous nellies, you fuddy-duddies, you windbags, you sitting ducks, you milquetoasts.* The speakers should strive for a certain acoustic uniformity. However, except for the acoustic pattern, no other picture should be produced. The invectives are not directed at anyone in particular. The manner of their delivery should not induce a meaning. The speakers reach the front of the stage before they finish rehearsing their invectives. They stand at ease but form a sort of pattern. They are not completely fixed in their positions but move according to the movement which the words they speak lend them. They now look at the public, but at no one person in particular. They are silent for a while. They collect themselves. Then they begin to speak. The order in which they speak is immaterial. The speakers have roughly the same amount of work to do.

You are welcome.

This piece is a prologue.

You will hear nothing you have not heard here before.
You will see nothing you have not seen here before.
You will see nothing of what you have always seen here.
You will hear nothing of what you have always heard here.

You will hear what you usually see.
You will hear what you usually don't see.
You will see no spectacle.
Your curiosity will not be satisfied.
You will see no play.
There will be no playing here tonight.
You will see a spectacle without pictures.

You expected something.
You expected something else perhaps.
You expected objects.
You expected no objects.
You expected an atmosphere.
You expected a different world.
You expected no different world.
In any case, you expected something.
It may be the case that you expected what you are hearing now.
But even in that case you expected something different.

You are sitting in rows. You form a pattern. You are sitting in a certain order. You are facing in a certain direction. You are sitting equidistant from one another. You are an audience. You form a unit. You are auditors and spectators in an auditorium. Your thoughts are free. You can still make up your own mind. You see us speaking and you hear us speaking. You are beginning to breathe in one and the same rhythm. You are beginning to breathe in one and the same rhythm in which we are speaking. You are breathing the way we are speaking. We and you gradually form a unit.

You are not thinking. You don't think of anything. You are thinking along. You are not thinking along. You feel uninhibited. Your thoughts are free. Even as we say that, we insinuate ourselves into your thoughts. You have thoughts in the back of your mind. Even as we say that, we insinuate ourselves into the thoughts in back of your mind. You are thinking along. You are hearing. Your thoughts are following in the track of our thoughts. Your thoughts are not following in the track of our thoughts. You are not thinking. Your thoughts are not free. You feel inhibited.

You are looking at us when we speak to you. You are not watching us. You are looking at us. You are being looked at. You are unprotected. You no longer have the advantage of looking from the shelter of darkness into the light. We no longer have the disadvantage of looking through the blinding light into the dark. You are not watching. You are looking at and you are being looked at. In this way, we and you gradually form a unit. Under certain conditions, therefore, we, instead of saying *you*, could say *we*. We are under one and the same roof. We are a closed society.

You are not listening to us. You heed us. You are no longer eavesdropping from behind a wall. We are speaking directly to you. Our dialogue no longer moves at a right angle to your glance. Your glance no longer pierces our dialogue. Our words and your glances no longer form an angle. You are not disregarded. You are not treated as mere hecklers. You need not form an opinion from a bird's or a frog's perspective of anything that happens here. You need not play referee. You are no longer treated as spectators to whom we can speak in asides. This is no play. There are no asides here. Nothing that takes place here is intended as an appeal to you. This is no play. We don't step out of the play to address you. We have no need of illusions to disillusion you. We show you nothing. We are playing no destinies. We are playing no dreams. This is not a factual report. This is no documentary play. This is no slice of life. We don't tell you a story. We don't perform any actions. We don't simulate any actions. We don't represent anything. We don't put anything on for you. We only speak. We play by addressing you. When we say we, we may also mean you. We are not acting out your situation. You cannot recognize yourselves in us. We are playing no situation. You need not feel that we mean you. You cannot feel that we mean you. No mirror is being held up to you. We don't mean you. We are addressing you. You are being addressed. You will be addressed. You will be bored if you don't want to be addressed.

You are sharing no experience. You are not sharing. You are not following suit. You are experiencing no intrigues here. You are experiencing nothing. You are not imagining anything. You don't have to imagine anything. You need no prerequisites. You don't need to know that this is a stage. You need no expectations. You need not lean back expectantly. You don't need to know that this is only playing. We make up no stories. You are not following an event. You are not playing along. You are being played with here. That is a wordplay.

What is the theater's is not rendered unto the theater here. Here you don't receive your due. Your curiosity is not satisfied. No spark will leap across from us to you. You will not be electrified. These boards don't signify a world. They are part of the world. These boards exist for us to stand on. This world is no different from yours. You are no longer kibitzers. You are the subject matter. The focus is on you. You are in the crossfire of our words.

OFFENDING THE AUDIENCE

This is no mirage. You don't see walls that tremble. You don't hear the spurious sounds of doors snapping shut. You hear no sofas squeaking. You see no apparitions. You have no visions. You see no picture of something. Nor do you see the suggestion of a picture. You see no picture puzzle. Nor do you see an empty picture. The emptiness of this stage is no picture of another emptiness. The emptiness of this stage signifies nothing. This stage is empty because objects would be in our way. It is empty because we don't need objects. This stage represents nothing. It represents no other emptiness. This stage *is* empty. You don't see any objects that pretend to be other objects. You don't see a darkness that pretends to be another darkness. You don't see a brightness that pretends to be another brightness. You don't see any light that pretends to be another light. You don't hear any noise that pretends to be another noise. You don't see a room that pretends to be another room. Here you are not experiencing a time that pretends to be another time. The time on stage is no different from the time off stage. We have the same local time here. We are in the same location. We are breathing the same air. The stage apron is not a line of demarcation. It is not only sometimes no demarcation line. It is no demarcation line as long as we are speaking to you. There is no invisible circle here. There is no magic circle. There is no room for play here. We are not playing. We are all in the same room. The demarcation line has not been penetrated, it is not pervious, it doesn't even exist. There is no radiation belt between you and us. We are not self-propelled props. We are no pictures of something. We are no representatives. We represent nothing. We demonstrate nothing. We have no pseudonyms. Our heartbeat does not pretend to be another's heartbeat. Our bloodcurdling screams don't pretend to be another's bloodcurdling screams. We don't step out of our roles. We have no roles. We are ourselves. We are the mouthpiece of the author. You cannot make yourself a picture of us. You don't need to make yourself a picture of us. We are ourselves. Our opinion and the author's opinion are not necessarily the same.

The light that illuminates us signifies nothing. Neither do the clothes we wear signify anything. They indicate nothing, they are not unusual in any way, they signify nothing. They signify no other time to you, no other climate, no other season, no other degree of latitude, no other reason to wear them. They have no function. Nor do our gestures have a function, that is, to signify something to you. This is not the world as a stage.

We are no slapstick artists. There are no objects here that we might trip over. Insidious objects are not on the program. Insidious objects are not spoil-sports because we are not sporting with them. The objects are not intended as insidious sport; they are insidious. If we happen to trip, we trip unwittingly. Unwitting as well are mistakes in dress; unwitting, too, are our perhaps foolish faces. Slips of the tongue, which amuse you, are not intended. If we stutter, we stutter without meaning to. We cannot make dropping a handkerchief part of the play. We are not playing. We cannot make the insidiousness of objects part of the play. We cannot camouflage the insidiousness of objects. We cannot be of two minds. We cannot be of many minds.We are no clowns. We are not in an arena. You don't have the pleasure of encircling us. You are not enjoying the comedy of having a rear view of us. You are not enjoying the comedy of insidious objects. You are enjoying the comedy of words.

The possibilities of the theater are not exploited here. The realm of possibilities is not exhausted. The theater is not unbounded. The theater is bound. Fate is meant ironically here. We are not theatrical. Our comedy is not overwhelming. Your laughter cannot be liberating. We are not playful. We are not playing a world for you. This is not half of one world. We and you do not constitute two halves.

OFFENDING THE AUDIENCE

You are the subject matter. You are the center of interest. No actions are performed here, you are being acted upon. That is no wordplay. You are not treated as individuals here. You don't become individuals here. You have no individual traits. You have no distinctive physiognomies. You are not individuals here. You have no characteristics. You have no destiny. You have no history. You have no past. You are on no wanted list. You have no experience of life. You have the experience of the theater here. You have that certain something. You are playgoers. You are of no interest because of your capacities. You are of interest solely in your capacity as playgoers. As playgoers you form a pattern here. You are no personalities. You are not singular. You are a plurality of persons. Your faces point in one direction. You are an event. You are *the* event.

You are under review by us. But you form no picture. You are not symbolic. You are an ornament. You are a pattern. You have features that everyone here has. You have general features. You are a species. You form a pattern. You are doing and you are not doing the same thing: you are looking in one direction. You don't stand up and look in different directions. You are a standard pattern and you have a pattern as a standard. You have a standard with which you came to the theater. You have the standard idea that where we are is up and where you are is down. You have the standard idea of two worlds. You have the standard idea of the world of the theater.

You don't need this standard now. You are not attending a piece for the theater. You are not attending. You are the focal point. You are in the crossfire. You are being inflamed. You can catch fire. You don't need a standard. You are the standard. You have been discovered. You are the discovery of the evening. You inflame us. Our words catch fire on you. From you a spark leaps across to us.

This room does not make believe it is a room. The side that is open to you is not the fourth wall of a house. The world does not have to be cut open here. You don't see any doors here. You don't see the two doors of the old dramas. You don't see the back door through which he who shouldn't be seen can slip out. You don't see the front door through which he who wants to see him who shouldn't be seen enters. There is no back door. Neither is there a nonexistent door as in modern drama. The nonexistent door does not represent a nonexistent door. This is not another world. We are not pretending that you don't exist. You are not thin air for us. You are of crucial importance to us because you exist. We are speaking to you because you exist. If you did not exist, we would be speaking to thin air. Your existence is not simply taken for granted. You don't watch us through a keyhole. We don't pretend that we are alone in the world. We don't explain ourselves to ourselves only in order to put you in the know. We are not conducting an exhibition purely for the benefit of your enlightenment. We need no artifice to enlighten you. We need no tricks. We don't have to be the-atrically effective. We have no entrances, we have no exits, we don't talk to you in asides. We are putting nothing over on you. We are not about to enter into a dialogue. We are not in a dialogue. Nor are we in a dialogue with you. We have no wish to enter into a dialogue with you. You are not in collusion with us. You are not eyewitnesses to an event. We are not taunting you. You don't have to be apathetic any more. You don't have to watch inactively any more. No actions take place here. You feel the discomfort of being watched and addressed, since you came prepared to watch and make yourselves comfortable in the shelter of the dark. Your pres-ence is every moment explicitly acknowledged with every one of our words. Your presence is the topic we deal with from one breath to the next, from one moment to the next, from one word to the next. Your standard idea of the theater is no longer presupposed as the basis of our actions. You are neither condemned to watch nor free to watch. You are the subject. You are the playmakers. You are the counterplotters. You are being aimed at. You are the target of our words. You serve as targets. That is a metaphor. You serve as the target of our metaphors. You serve as metaphors.

Of the two poles here, you are the pole at rest. You are in an arrested state. You find yourself in a state of expectation. You are no subjects. You are objects here. You are the objects of our words. Still, you are subjects too.

There are no intervals here. The intervals between words lack significance. Here the unspoken word lacks significance. There are no unspoken words here. Our silences say nothing. There is no deafening silence. There is no silent silence. There is no deathly quiet. Speech is not used to create silence here. This play includes no direction telling us to be silent. We make no artificial pauses. Our pauses are natural pauses. Our pauses are not eloquent like speech. We say nothing with our silence. No abyss opens up between words. You cannot read anything between our lines. You cannot read anything in our faces. Our gestures express nothing of consequence to anything. What is inexpressible is not said through silences here. Glances and gestures are not eloquent here. Becoming silent and being silent is no artifice here. There are no silent letters here. There's only the mute *h*. That is a pun.

You have made up your mind now. You recognized that we negate something. You recognized that we repeat ourselves. You recognized that we contradict ourselves. You recognized that this piece is conducting an argument with the theater. You recognized the dialectical structure of the piece. You recognized a certain spirit of contrariness. The intention of the piece became clear to you. You recognized that we primarily negate. You recognized that we repeat ourselves. You recognize. You see through. You have not made up your mind. You have not seen through the dialectical structure of the piece. Now you are seeing through. Your thoughts were one thought too slow. Now you have thoughts in the back of your mind.

You look charming. You look enchanting. You look dazzling. You look breathtaking. You look unique.

But you don't make an evening. You're not a brilliant idea. You are tiresome. You are not a thankful subject. You are a theatrical blunder. You are not true to life. You are not theatrically effective. You don't send us. You don't enchant us. You don't dazzle us. You don't entertain us fabulously. You are not playful. You are not sprightly. You have no tricks up your sleeve. You have no nose for the theater. You have nothing to say. Your debut is unconvincing. You are not with it. You don't help us pass the time. You are not addressing the human quality in us. You leave us cold.

This is no drama. No action that has occurred elsewhere is re-enacted here. Only a now and a now and a now exist here. This is no make-believe which re-enacts an action that really happened once upon a time. Time plays no role here. We are not acting out a plot. Therefore we are not playing time. Time is for real here, it expires from one word to the next. Time flies in the words here. It is not alleged that time can be repeated here. No play can be repeated here and play at the same time it did once upon a time. The time here is *your* time. Space time here is your space time. Here you can compare your time with our time. Time is no noose. That is no make-believe. It is not alleged here that time can be repeated. The umbilical cord connecting you to your time is not severed here. Time is not at play here. We mean business with time here. It is admitted here that time expires from one word to the next. It is admitted that this is your time here. You can check the time here on your watches. No other time governs here. The time that governs here is measured against your breath. Time conforms to your wishes here. We measure time by your breath, by the batting of your eyelashes, by your pulsebeats, by the growth of your cells. Time expires here from moment to moment. Time is measured in moments. Time is measured in your moments. Time goes through your stomach. Time here is not repeatable as in the make-believe of a theater performance. This is no performance: you have not to imagine anything. Time is no noose here. Time is not cut off from the outside world here. There are no two levels of time here. There are no two worlds here. While we are here, the earth continues to turn. Our time up here is your time down there. It expires from one word to the next. It expires while we, we and you, are breathing, while our hair is growing, while we are sweating, while we are smelling, while we are hearing. Time is not repeatable even if we repeat our words, even if we mention again that our time is your time, that it expires from one word to the next, while we, we and you, are breathing, while our hair is growing, while we sweat, while we smell, while we hear. We cannot repeat anything, time is expiring. It is unrepeatable. Each moment is historical. Each of your moments is a historical moment. We cannot say our words twice. This is no make-believe. We cannot do the same thing once again. We cannot repeat the same gestures. We cannot speak the same way. Time expires on our lips. Time is unrepeatable. Time is no noose. That is no make-believe. The past is not made contemporaneous. The past is dead and buried. We need no puppet to embody a dead time. This is no puppet show. This is no nonsense. This is no play. This is no sense. You recognize the contradiction. Time here serves the wordplay.

This is no maneuver. This is no exercise for the emergency. No one has to play dead here. No one has to pretend he is alive. Nothing is posited here. The number of wounded is not prescribed. The result is not predetermined on paper. There is no result here. No one has to present himself here. We don't represent except what we are. We don't represent ourselves in a state other than the one we are in now and here. This is no maneuver. We are not playing ourselves in different situations. We are not thinking of the emergency. We don't have to represent our death. We don't have to represent our life. We don't play ahead of time what and how we will be. We make no future contemporaneous in our play. We don't represent another time. We don't represent the emergency. We are speaking while time expires. We speak of the expiration of time. We are not doing as if. We are not doing as if we could repeat time or as if we could anticipate time. This is neither make-believe nor a maneuver. On the one hand we do as if. We do as if we could repeat words. We appear to repeat ourselves. Here is the world of appearances. Here appearance is appearance. Appearance is here appearance.

You represent something. You are someone. You are something. You are not someone here but something. You are a society that represents an order. You are a theater society of sorts. You are an order because of your kind of dress, the position of your bodies, the direction of your glances. The color of your clothes clashes with the color of your seating arrangement. You also form an order with the seating arrangement. You are dressed up. With your dress you observe an order. You dress up. By dressing up, you demonstrate that you are doing something that you don't do every day. You are putting on a masquerade so as to partake of a masquerade. You partake. You watch. You stare. By watching, you become rigid. The seating arrangement favors this development. You are something that watches. You need room for your eyes. If the curtain comes together, you gradually become claustrophobic. You have no vantage point. You feel encircled. You feel inhibited. The parting of the curtain merely relieves your claustrophobia. Thus it relieves you. You can watch. Your view is unobstructed. You become uninhibited. You can partake. You are not in dead center as when the curtain is closed. You are no longer someone. You become something. You are no longer alone with yourselves. You are no longer left to your own devices. Now you are with it. You are an audience. That is a relief. You can partake.

OFFENDING THE AUDIENCE

Up here there is no order now. There are no objects that demonstrate an order to you. The world here is neither sound nor unsound. This is no world. Stage props are out of place here. Their places are not chalked out on the stage. Since they are not chalked out, there is no order here. There are no chalk marks for the standpoint of things. There are no memory props for the standpoint of persons. In contrast to you and your seating arrangement, nothing is in its place here. Things here have no fixed places like the places of your seating arrangements down there. This stage is no world, just as the world is no stage.

Nor does each thing have its own time here. No thing has its own time here. No thing has its fixed time here when it serves as a prop or when it becomes an obstacle. We don't do as if things were really used. Here things *are* useful.

You are not standing. You are using the seating arrangements. You are sitting. Since your seating arrangements form a pattern, you form a pattern as well. There is no standing-room. People enjoy art more effectively when they sit than if they stand. That is why you are sitting. You are friendlier when you sit. You are more receptive. You are more open-minded. You are more long-suffering. Sitting, you are more relaxed. You are more democratic. You are less bored. Time seems less long and boring to you. You allow more to happen with yourself. You are more clairvoyant. You are less distracted. It is easier for you to forget your surroundings. The world around you disappears more easily. You begin to resemble one another more. You begin to lose your personal qualities. You begin to lose the characteristics that distinguish you from each other. You become a unit. You become a pattern. You become one. You lose your self-consciousness. You become spectators. You become auditors. You become apathetic. You become all eyes and ears. You forget to look at your watch. You forget yourself.

Standing, you would be more effective hecklers. In view of the anatomy of the human body, your heckling would be louder if you stood. You would be better able to clench your fists. You could show your opposition better. You would have greater mobility. You would not need to be as well-behaved. You could shift your weight from one foot to the other. You could more easily become conscious of your body. Your enjoyment of art would be diminished. You would no longer form a pattern. You would no longer be rigid. You would lose your geometry. You would be better able to smell the sweat of the bodies near you. You would be better able to express agreement by nudging each other. If you stood, the sluggishness of your bodies would not keep you from walking. Standing, you would be more individual. You would oppose the theater more resolutely. You would give in to fewer illusions. You would suffer more from absentmindedness. You would stand more on the outside. You would be better able to leave yourself to your own devices. You would be less able to imagine represented events as real. The events here would seem less true to life to you. Standing, for example, you would be less able to imagine a death represented on this stage as real. You would be less rigid. You wouldn't let yourself be put under as much of a spell. You wouldn't let as much be put over on you. You wouldn't be satisfied to be mere spectators. It would be easier for you to be of two minds. You could be at two places at once with your thoughts. You could live in two space-time continuums.

We don't want to infect you. We don't want to goad you into a show of feelings. We don't play feelings. We don't embody feelings. We neither laugh nor weep. We don't want to infect you with laughter by laughing or with weeping by laughing or with laughter by weeping or with weeping by weeping. Although laughter is more infectious than weeping, we don't infect you with laughter by laughing. And so forth. We are not playing. We play nothing. We don't modulate. We don't gesticulate. We express ourselves by no

OFFENDING THE AUDIENCE

means but words. We only speak. We express. We don't express ourselves but the opinion of the author. We express ourselves by speaking. Our speaking is our acting. By speaking, we become theatrical. We are theatrical because we are speaking in a theater. By always speaking directly to you and by speaking to you of time, of now and of now and of now, we observe the unity of time, place, and action. But we observe this unity not only here on stage. Since the stage is no world unto itself, we also observe the unity down where you are. We and you form a unity because we speak directly to you without interruption. Therefore, under certain conditions, we, instead of saying you, could say we. That signifies the unity of action. The stage up here and the auditorium constitute a unity in that they no longer constitute two levels. There is no radiation belt between us. There are no two places here. Here is only one place. That signifies the unity of place. Your time, the time of the spectators and auditors, and our time, the time of the speakers, form a unity in that no other time passes here than your time. Time is not bisected here into played time and play time. Time is not played here. Only real time exists here. Only the time that we, we and you, experience ourselves in our own bodies exists here. Only one time exists here. That signifies the unity of time. All three cited circumstances, taken together, signify the unity of time, place, and action. Therefore this piece is classical.

Because we speak to you, you can become conscious of yourself. Because we speak to you, your self-awareness increases. You become aware that you are sitting. You become aware that you are sitting in a theater. You become aware of the size of your limbs. You become aware of how your limbs are situated. You become aware of your fingers. You become aware of your tongue. You become aware of your throat. You become aware how heavy your head is. You become aware of your sex organs. You become aware of batting your eyelids. You become aware of the muscles with which you swallow. You become aware of the flow of your saliva. You become aware of the beating of your heart. You become aware of raising your eyebrows. You become aware of a prickling sensation on your scalp. You become aware of the impulse to scratch yourself. You become aware of sweating under your armpits. You become aware of your sweaty hands. You become aware of your parched hands. You become aware of the air you are inhaling and exhaling through your mouth and nose. You become aware of our words entering your ears. You acquire presence of mind.

Try not to blink your eyelids. Try not to swallow any more. Try not to move your tongue. Try not to hear anything. Try not to smell anything. Try not to salivate. Try not to sweat. Try not to shift in your seat. Try not to breathe.

Why, you are breathing. Why, you are salivating. Why, you are listening. Why, you are smelling. Why, you are swallowing. Why, you are blinking your eyelids. Why, you are belching. Why, you are sweating. Why, how terribly self-conscious you are.

Don't blink. Don't salivate. Don't bat your eyelashes. Don't inhale. Don't exhale. Don't shift in your seat. Don't listen to us. Don't smell. Don't swallow. Hold your breath.

Swallow. Salivate. Blink. Listen. Breathe.

You are now aware of your presence. You know that it is *your* time that you are spending here. You are the topic. You tie the knot. You untie the knot. You are the center. You are the occasion. You are the reasons why. You provide the initial impulse. You provide us with words here. You are the playmakers and the counterplotters. You are the youthful comedians. You are the youthful lovers, you are the ingénues, you are the sentimentalists. You are the stars, you are the character actors, you are the bon vivants and the heroes. You are the heroes and the villains of this piece.

OFFENDING THE AUDIENCE

Before you came here, you made certain preparations. You came here with certain preconceptions. You went to the theater. You prepared yourself to go to the theater. You had certain expectations. Your thoughts were one step ahead of time. You imagined something. You prepared yourself for something. You prepared yourself to partake in something. You prepared yourself to be seated, to sit on the rented seat and to attend something. Perhaps you had heard of this piece. So you made preparations, you prepared yourself for something. You let events come toward you. You were prepared to sit and have something shown to you.

The rhythm you breathed in was different from ours. You went about dressing yourself in a different manner. You got started in a different way. You approached this location from different directions. You used the public transportation system. You came on foot. You came by cab. You used your own means of transportation. Before you got underway, you looked at your watch. You expected a telephone call, you picked up the receiver, you turned on the lights, you turned out the lights, you closed doors, you turned keys, you stepped out into the open. You propelled your legs. You let your arms swing up and down as you walked. You walked. You walked from different directions all in the same direction. You found your way here with the help of your sense of direction.

Because of your plan you distinguished yourselves from others who were on their way to other locations. Simply because of your plan, you instantly formed a unit with the others who were on their way to this location. You had the same objective. You planned to spend a part of your future together with others at a definite time.

You crossed traffic lanes. You looked left and right. You observed traffic signals. You nodded to others. You stopped. You informed others of your destination. You told of your expectations. You communicated your speculations about this piece. You expressed your opinion of this piece. You shook hands. You had others wish you a pleasant evening. You took off your shoes. You held doors open. You had doors held open for you. You met other theatergoers. You felt like conspirators. You observed the rules of good behavior. You helped out of coats. You let yourselves be helped out of coats. You stood around. You walked around. You heard the buzzers. You grew restless. You looked in the mirror. You checked your makeup. You threw sidelong glances. You noticed sidelong glances. You walked. You paced. Your movements became more formal. You heard the buzzer. You looked at your watch. You became conspirators. You took your seat. You took a look around. You made yourself comfortable. You heard the buzzer. You stopped chatting. You aligned your glances. You raised your heads. You took a deep breath. You saw the lights dim. You became silent. You heard the doors closing. You stared at the curtain. You waited. You became rigid. You did not move any more. Instead, the curtain moved. You heard the curtain rustling. You were offered an unobstructed view of the stage. Everything was as it always is. Your expectations were not disappointed. You were ready. You leaned back in your seat. The play could begin.

At other times you were also ready. You were on to the game that was being played. You leaned back in your seats. You perceived. You followed. You pursued. You let happen. You let something happen up here that had happened long ago. You watched the past which by means of dialogue and monologue made believe it was contemporaneous. You let yourselves be captivated. You let yourselves become spellbound. You forgot where you were. You forgot the time. You became rigid and remained rigid. You did not move. You did not act. You did not even come up front to see better. You followed no natural impulses. You watched as you watch a beam of light that was produced long before you began to watch. You looked into dead space. You looked at dead points. You experienced a dead time. You heard a dead language. You yourselves were in a dead room in a dead time. It was dead calm. No breath of air moved. You did not move. You stared. The distance between you and us was infinite. We were infinitely far away from you. We moved at an infinite distance from you. We had lived infinitely long before you. We lived up here on the stage before the beginning of time. Your glances and our glances met in infinity. An infinite space was between us. We played. But we did not play with you. You were always posterity here.

Plays were played here. Sense was played here. Nonsense with meaning was played here. The plays here had a background and an underground. They had a false bottom. They were not what they were. They were not what they seemed. There was something in back of them. The things and the plot seemed to be, but they were not. They seemed to be as they seemed, but they were different. They did not seem to seem as in a pure play, they seemed to be. They seemed to be reality. The plays here did not pass the time, or they did not only pass the time. They had meaning. They were not timeless like the pure plays, an unreal time passed in them. The conspicuous meaninglessness of some plays was precisely what represented their hidden meaning. Even the pranks of pranksters acquired meaning on these boards. Always something lay in wait. Always something lay in ambush between the words, gestures, props and sought to mean something to you. Always something had two or more meanings. Something was always happening. Something happened in the play that you were supposed to think was real. Stories always happened. A played and unreal time happened. What you saw and heard was supposed to be not only what you saw and heard. It was supposed to be what you did not see and did not hear. Everything was meant. Everything expressed. Even what pretended to express nothing expressed something because something that happens in the theater expresses something. Everything that was played expressed something real. The play was not played for the play's sake but for the sake of reality. You were to discover a played reality behind the play. You were supposed to fathom the play. Not a play, reality was played.

Time was played. Since time was played, reality was played. The theater played tribunal. The theater played arena. The theater played moral institution. The theater played dreams. The theater played tribal rites. The theater played mirrors for you. The play exceeded the play. It hinted at reality. It became impure. It meant. Instead of time staying out of play, an unreal and uneffective time transpired. With the unreal time an unreal reality was played. It was not there, it was only signified to you, it was performed. Neither reality nor play transpired here. If a clean play had been played here, time could have been left out of play. A clean play has no time. But since a reality was played, the corresponding time was also played. If a clean play had been played here, there would have been only the time of the spectators here. But since reality was part of the play here, there were always two times: your time, the time of the spectators, and the played time, which seemed to be the real time. But time cannot be played. It cannot be repeated in any play. Time is irretrievable. Time is irresistible. Time is unplayable. Time is real. It cannot be played as real. Since time cannot be played, reality cannot be played either. Only a play where time is left out of play is a play. A play in which time plays a role is no play. Only a timeless play is without meaning. Only a timeless play is self-sufficient. Only a timeless play does not need to *play* time. Only for a timeless play is time without meaning. All other plays are impure plays. There are only plays without time, or plays in which time is real time, like the sixty minutes of a football game, which has only one time because the time of the players is the same time as that of the spectators. All other plays are sham plays. All other plays mirror meretricious facts for you. A timeless play mirrors no facts.

We could do a play within a play for you. We could act out happenings for you that are taking place outside this room during these moments while you are swallowing, while you are batting your eyelashes. We could illustrate the statistics. We could represent what is statistically taking place at other places while you are at this place. By representing what is happening, we could make you imagine these happenings. We could bring them closer to you. We would not need to represent anything that is past. We could play a clean game. For example, we could act out the very process of dying that is statistically happening somewhere at this moment. We could become full of pathos. We could declare that death is the pathos of time, of which we speak all the time. Death could be the pathos of this real time which you are wasting here. At the very least, this play within a play would help bring this piece to a dramatic climax.

But we are not putting anything over on you. We don't imitate. We don't represent any other persons and any other events, even if they statistically exist. We can do without a play of features and a play of gestures. There are no persons who are part of the plot and therefore no impersonators. The plot is not freely invented, for there is no plot. Since there is no plot, accidents are impossible. Similarity with still living or scarcely dead or long-dead persons is not accidental but impossible. For we don't represent anything and are no others than we are. We don't even play ourselves. We are speaking. Nothing is invented here. Nothing is imitated. Nothing is fact. Nothing is left to your imagination.

Due to the fact that we are not playing and not acting playfully, this piece is half as funny and half as tragic. Due to the fact that we only speak and don't fall outside time, we cannot depict anything for you and demonstrate nothing for you. We illustrate nothing. We conjure up nothing out of the past. We are not in conflict with the past. We are not in conflict with the present. We don't anticipate the future. In the present, the past, and the future, we speak of time.

That is why, for example, we cannot represent the now and now of dying that is statistically happening now. We cannot represent the gasping for breath that is happening now and now, or the tumbling and falling now, or the death throes, or the grinding of teeth now, or the last words, or the last sigh now, that is statistically happening now this very second, or the last exhalation, or the last ejaculation that is happening now, or the breathlessness that is statistically commencing now, and now, and now, and now, and so on, or the motionlessness now, or the statistically ascertainable rigor mortis, or the lying absolutely quiet now. We cannot represent it. We only speak of it. We are speaking of it *now*.

Due to the fact that we only speak and due to the fact that we don't speak of anything invented, we cannot be equivocal or ambiguous. Due to the fact that we play nothing, there cannot exist two or more levels here or a play within a play. Due to the fact that we don't gesticulate and don't tell you any stories and don't represent anything, we cannot be poetical. Due to the fact that we only speak to you, we lose the poetry of ambiguity. For example, we cannot use the gestures and expressions of dying that we mentioned to represent the gestures and expressions of a simultaneously transpiring instance of sexual intercourse that is statistically transpiring now. We can't be equivocal. We cannot play on a false bottom. We cannot remove ourselves from the world. We don't need to be poetic. We don't need to hypnotize you. We don't need to hoodwink you. We don't need to cast an evil eye on you. We don't need a second nature. This is no hypnosis. You don't have to imagine anything. You don't have to dream with open eyes. With the illogic of your dreams you are not dependent on the logic of the stage. The impossibilities of your dreams do not have to confine themselves to the possibilities of the stage. The absurdity of your dreams does not have to obey the authentic laws of the theater. Therefore we represent neither dreams nor reality. We make claims neither for life nor for dying, neither for society nor for the individual, neither for what is natural nor for what is supernatural, neither for lust nor for grief, neither for reality nor for the play. Time elicits no elegies from us.

OFFENDING THE AUDIENCE

This piece is a prologue. It is not the prologue to another piece but the prologue to what you did, what you are doing, and what you will do. You are the topic. This piece is the prologue to the topic. It is the prologue to your practices and customs. It is the prologue to your actions. It is the prologue to your inactivity. It is the prologue to your lying down, to your sitting, to your standing, to your walking. It is the prologue to the plays and to the seriousness of your life. It is also the prologue to your future visits to the theater. It is also the prologue to all other prologues. This piece is world theater.

Soon you will move. You will make preparations. You will prepare yourself to applaud. You will prepare yourself not to applaud. When you prepare to do the former, you will clap one hand against the other, that is to say, you will clap one palm to the other palm and repeat these claps in rapid succession. Meanwhile, you will be able to watch your hands clapping or not clapping. You will hear the sound of yourself clapping and the sound of clapping next to you and you will see next to you and in front of you the clapping hands bobbing back and forth or you will not hear the expected clapping and not see the hands bobbing back and forth. Instead, you will perhaps hear other sounds and will yourself produce other sounds. You will prepare to get up. You will hear the seats folding up behind you. You will see us taking our bows. You will see the curtain come together. You will be able to designate the noises the curtain makes during this process. You will pocket your programs. You will exchange glances. You will exchange words. You will get moving. You will make comments and hear comments. You will suppress comments. You will smile meaningfully. You will smile meaninglessly. You will push in an orderly fashion into the foyer. You will show your hatchecks to redeem your hats and coats. You will stand around. You will see yourselves in mirrors. You will help each other into coats. You will hold doors open for each other. You will say your goodbyes. You will accompany. You will be accompanied. You will step into the open. You will return into the everyday. You will go in different directions. If you remain together, you will be a theater party. You will go to a restaurant. You will think of tomorrow. You will gradually find your way back into reality. You will be able to call reality harsh again. You will be sobered up. You will lead your own lives again. You will no longer be a unit. You will go from one place to different places.

But before you leave you will be offended.

We will offend you because offending you is also one way of speaking to you. By offending you, we can be straight with you. We can switch you on. We can eliminate the free play. We can tear down a wall. We can observe you.

While we are offending you, you won't just hear us, you will listen to us. The distance between us will no longer be infinite. Due to the fact that we're offending you, your motionlessness and your rigidity will finally become overt. But we won't offend *you*, we will merely use offensive words which you yourselves use. We will contradict ourselves with our offenses. We will mean no one in particular. We will only create an acoustic pattern. You won't have to feel offended. You were warned in advance, so you can feel quite unoffended while we're offending you. Since you are probably thoroughly offended already, we will waste no more time before thoroughly offending you, you chuckleheads.

You let the impossible become possible. You were the heroes of this piece. You were sparing with your gestures. Your parts were well rounded. Your scenes were unforgettable. You did not play, you *were* the part. You were a happening. You were the find of the evening. You lived your roles. You had a lion's share of the success. You saved the piece. You were a sight. You were a sight to have seen, you ass-kissers.

OFFENDING THE AUDIENCE

You were always with it. Your honest toiling didn't help the piece a bit. You contributed only the cues. The best you created was the little you left out. Your silences said everything, you small-timers.

You were thoroughbred actors. You began promisingly. You were true to life. You were realistic. You put everything under your spell. You played us off the stage. You reached Shakespearean heights, you jerks, you hoodlums, you scum of the melting pot.

Not one wrong note crossed your lips. You had control of every scene. Your playing was of exquisite nobility. Your countenances were of rare exquisiteness. You were a smashing cast. You were a dream cast. You were inimitable, your faces unforgettable. Your sense of humor left us gasping. Your tragedy was of antique grandeur. You gave your best, you party-poopers, you freeloaders, you fuddy-duddies, you bubbleheads, you powder puffs, you sitting ducks.

You were one of a kind. You had one of your better days tonight. You played ensemble. You were imitations of life, you drips, you diddlers, you atheists, you double-dealers, you switch-hitters, you dirty Jews.

You showed us brand-new vistas. You were well advised to do this piece. You outdid yourselves. You played yourselves loose. You turned yourselves inside out, you lonely crowd, you culture vultures, you nervous nellies, you bronco busters, you moneybags, you potheads, you washouts, you wet smacks, you fire eaters, you generation of freaks, you hopped-up sons and daughters of the revolution, you napalm specialists.

You were priceless. You were a hurricane. You drove shudders up our spines. You swept everything before you, you Vietnam bandits, you savages, you rednecks, you hatchet men, you subhumans, you fiends, you beasts in human shape, you killer pigs.

You were the right ones. You were breathtaking. You did not disappoint our wildest hopes. You were born actors. Play-acting was in your blood, you butchers, you buggers, you bullshitters, you bullies, you rabbits, you fuck-offs, you farts.

You had perfect breath-control, you windbags, you waspish wasps, you wags, you gargoyles, you tackheads, you milquetoasts, you mickey-mice, you chicken-shits, you cheap skates, you wrong numbers, you zeros, you back numbers, you one-shots, you centipedes, you supernumeraries, you superfluous lives, you crumbs, you cardboard figures, you *pain* in the mouth.

You are accomplished actors, you hucksters, you traitors to your country, you grafters, you would-be revolutionaries, you reactionaries, you draft-card burners, you ivory-tower artists, you defeatists, you massive retaliators, you white-rabbit pacifists, you nihilists, you individualists, you Communists, you vigilantes, you socialists, you minute men, you whizz-kids, you turtledoves, you crazy hawks, you stool pigeons, you worms, you antediluvian monstrosities, you claquers, you clique of babbits, you rabble, you blubber, you quivering reeds, you wretches, you ofays, you oafs, you spooks, you blackbaiters, you cooky pushers, you abortions, you bitches and bastards, you nothings, you thingamajigs.

O you cancer victims, O you hemorrhoid sufferers, O you multiple sclerotics, O you syphilitics, O you cardiac conditions, O you paraplegics, O you catatonics, O you schizoids, O you paranoids, O you hypochondriacs, O you carriers of causes of death, O you suicide candidates, O you potential peacetime casualties, O you potential war dead, O you potential accident victims, O you potential increase in the mortality rate, O you potential dead.

You wax figures. You impersonators. You bad-hats. You troupers. You tear-jerkers. You potboilers. You foul mouths. You sell-outs.

OFFENDING THE AUDIENCE

You deadbeats. You phonies. You milestones in the history of the theater. You historic moments. You immortal souls. You positive heroes. You abortionists. You anti-heroes. You everyday heroes. You luminaries of science. You beacons in the dark. You educated gasbags. You cultivated classes. You befuddled aristocrats. You rotten middle class. You lowbrows. You people of our time. You children of the world. You sadsacks. You church and lay dignitaries. You wretches. You congressmen. You commissioners. You scoundrels. You generals. You lobbyists. You Chiefs of Staff. You chairmen of this and that. You tax evaders. You presidential advisers. You U-2 pilots. You agents. You corporate-military establishment. You entrepreneurs. You Eminencies. You Excellencies. You Holiness. Mr. President. You crowned heads. You pushers. You architects of the future. You builders of a better world. You mafiosos. You wiseacres. You smarty-pants. You who embrace life. You who detest life. You who have no feeling about life. You ladies and gents you, you celebrities of public and cultural life you, you who are present you, you brothers and sisters you, you comrades you, you worthy listeners you, you fellow humans you.

You were welcome here. We thank you. Good night.

[*The curtain comes together at once. However, it does not remain closed but parts again immediately regardless of the behavior of the public. The speakers stand and look at the public without looking at anyone in particular. Roaring applause and wild whistling is piped in through the loudspeakers; to this, one might add taped audience reactions to pop-music concerts. The deafening howling and yelling lasts until the public begins to leave. Only then does the curtain come together once and for all.*]

SELF-ACCUSATION

for Libgart

This piece is a Sprechstück *for one male and one female speaker. It has no roles. Female and male speaker, whose voices are attuned to each other, alternate or speak together, quiet and loud, with abrupt transitions, thus producing an acoustic order. The stage is empty. The two speakers use microphones and loudspeakers. The auditorium and the stage are lighted throughout. The curtain is not used at any time, not even at the end of the piece.*

I came into the world.

I became. I was begotten. I originated. I grew. I was born. I was entered in the birth register. I grew older.

I moved. I moved parts of my body. I moved my body. I moved on one and the same spot. I moved from the spot. I moved from one spot to another. I had to move. I was able to move.

I moved my mouth. I came to my senses. I made myself noticeable. I screamed. I spoke. I heard noises. I distinguished between noises. I produced noises. I produced sounds. I produced tones. I was able to produce tones, noises, and sounds. I was able to speak. I was able to scream. I was able to remain silent.

I saw. I saw what I had seen before. I became conscious. I recognized what I had seen before. I recognized what I had recognized before. I perceived. I perceived what I had perceived before. I became conscious. I recognized what I had perceived before.

I looked. I saw objects. I looked at indicated objects. I indicated indicated objects. I learned the designation of indicated objects. I designated indicated objects. I learned the designation of objects that cannot be indicated. I learned. I remembered. I remembered the signs I learned. I saw designated forms. I designated similar forms with the same name. I designated differences between dissimilar forms. I designated absent forms. I learned to fear absent forms. I learned to wish for the presence of absent forms. I learned the words "to wish" and "to fear."

SELF-ACCUSATION

I learned. I learned the words. I learned the verbs. I learned the difference between being and having been. I learned the nouns. I learned the difference between singular and plural. I learned the adverbs. I learned the difference between here and there. I learned the demonstrative pronouns. I learned the difference between this and that. I learned the adjectives. I learned the difference between good and evil. I learned the possessives. I learned the difference between mine and yours. I acquired a vocabulary.

I became the object of sentences. I became the supplement of sentences. I became the object and the supplement of principle and subordinate clauses. I became the movement of a mouth. I became a sequence of letters of the alphabet.

I said my name. I said I. I crawled on all fours. I ran. I ran toward something. I ran away from something. I stood up. I stepped out of the passive form. I became active. I walked at approximately a right angle to the earth. I leapt. I defied the force of gravity. I learned to relieve myself outside my clothes. I learned to bring my body under my control. I learned to control myself.

I learned to be able. I was able. I was able to want. I was able to walk on two legs. I was able to walk on my hands. I was able to remain. I was able to remain upright. I was able to remain prone. I was able to crawl on my stomach. I was able to play dead. I was able to hold my breath. I was able to kill myself. I was able to spit. I was able to nod. I was able to say no. I was able to perform gestures. I was able to question. I was able to answer questions. I was able to imitate. I was able to follow an example. I was able to play. I was able to do something. I was able to fail to do something. I was able to destroy objects. I was able to picture objects to myself. I was able to value objects. I was able to speak objects. I was able to speak about objects. I was able to remember objects.

I lived in time. I thought of beginning and end. I thought of myself. I thought of others. I stepped out of nature. I became. I became unnatural. I came to my history. I recognized that I am not you. I was able to tell my history. I was able to conceal my history.

I was able to want something. I was able not to want something.

I made myself. I made myself what I am. I changed myself. I became someone else. I became responsible for my history. I became co-responsible for the histories of the others. I became one history among others. I made the world into my own. I became sensible.

I no longer had to obey only nature. I was supposed to comply with rules. I was supposed to. I was supposed to comply with mankind's historic rules. I was supposed to act. I was supposed to fail to act. I was supposed to let happen. I learned rules. I learned as a metaphor for rules "the snares of rules." I learned rules for behavior and for thoughts. I learned rules for inside and outside. I learned rules for things and people. I learned general and specific rules. I learned rules for this world and the afterworld. I learned rules for air, water, fire, and earth. I learned the rules and the exceptions to the rules. I learned the basic rules and the derivative rules. I learned to pretend. I became fit for society.

I became: I was supposed to. I became capable of eating with my hands: I was supposed to avoid soiling myself. I became capable of adopting other people's practices: I was supposed to avoid my own malpractices. I became capable of distinguishing between hot and cold: I was supposed to avoid playing with fire. I became capable of separating good and evil: I was supposed to eschew evil. I became capable of playing according to the rules: I was supposed to avoid an infraction of the rules of the game. I became capable of realizing the unlawfulness of my actions and of acting in accordance with

SELF-ACCUSATION

this realization: I was supposed to eschew criminal acts. I became capable of using my sexual powers: I was supposed to avoid misusing my sexual powers.

I was included in all the rules. With my personal data I became part of the record. With my soul I became tainted by original sin. With my lottery number I was inscribed in the lottery lists. With my illnesses I was filed in the hospital ledger. With my firm I was entered in the commercial register. With my distinguishing marks I was retained in the personnel records.

I came of age. I became fit to act. I became fit to sign a contract. I became fit to have a last will.

As of a moment in time I could commit sins. As of another moment I became liable to prosecution. As of another moment I could loose my honor. As of another moment I could oblige myself contractually to do or to abstain from doing something.

I became duty-bound to confess. I became duty-bound to have an address. I became duty-bound to make restitution. I became duty-bound to pay taxes. I became duty-bound to do military service. I became duty-bound to do my duty. I became duty-bound to go to school. I became duty-bound to be vaccinated. I became duty-bound to care. I became duty-bound to pay my bills. I became duty-bound to be investigated. I became duty-bound to be educated. I became duty-bound to give proof. I became duty-bound to be insured. I became duty-bound to have an identity. I became duty-bound to be registered. I became duty-bound to pay support. I became duty-bound to execute. I became duty-bound to testify.

I became. I became responsible. I became guilty. I became pardonable. I had to atone for my history. I had to atone for my past. I had to atone for the past. I had to atone for my time. I came into the world only with time.

Which demands of time did I violate? Which demands of practical reason did I violate? Which secret paragraphs did I violate? Which programs did I violate? Which eternal laws of the universe did I violate? Which laws of the underworld did I violate? Which of the most primitive rules of common decency did I violate? Which and whose party lines did I violate? Which laws of the theater did I violate? Which vital interests did I violate? Which unspoken law did I violate? Which unwritten law did I violate? Which command of the hour did I violate? Which rules of life did I violate? Which common-sense rules did I violate? Which rules of love did I violate? Which rules of the game did I violate? Which rules of cosmetics did I violate? Which laws of aesthetics did I violate? Which laws of the stronger did I violate? Which commands of piety did I violate? Which law of the outlaws did I violate? Which desire for change did I violate? Which law of the world and the afterworld did I violate? Which rule of orthography did I violate? Which right of the past did I violate? Which law of free fall did I violate? Did I violate the rules, plans, ideas, postulates, basic principles, etiquettes, general propositions, opinions, and formulas of the whole world?

I did. I failed to do. I let do. I expressed myself. I expressed myself through ideas. I expressed myself through expressions. I expressed myself before myself. I expressed myself before myself and others. I expressed myself before the impersonal power of the law and of good conduct. I expressed myself before the personal power of God.

I expressed myself in movements. I expressed myself in actions. I expressed myself in motionlessness. I expressed myself in inaction.

I signified. I signified with each of my expressions. With each of my expressions I signified the fulfillment or disregard of rules.

SELF-ACCUSATION

I expressed myself by spitting. I expressed myself by showing disapproval. I expressed myself by showing approval. I expressed myself by relieving nature. I expressed myself by discarding useless and used objects. I expressed myself by killing live beings. I expressed myself by destroying objects. I expressed myself by breathing. I expressed myself by sweating. I expressed myself by secreting snot and tears.

I spat. I spat out. I spat with an aim. I spat at. I spat on the floor in places where it was improper to spit on the floor. I spat on the floor in places where spitting was a violation of health regulations. I spat in the face of people whom it was a personal insult of God to spit at. I spat on objects which it was a personal insult of human beings to spit upon. I did not spit in front of people when spitting out before them allegedly brought good luck. I did not spit in front of cripples. I did not spit at actors before their performance. I did not use the spittoon. I expectorated in waiting rooms. I spat against the wind.

I expressed approval in places where the expression of approval was prohibited. I expressed disapproval at times when the expression of disapproval was not desired. I expressed disapproval and approval in places and at times when the expression of disapproval and the expression of approval were intolerable. I failed to express approval at times when the expression of approval was called for. I expressed approval during a difficult trapeze act in the circus. I expressed approval inopportunely.

I discarded used and useless objects in places where discarding objects was prohibited. I deposited objects in places where depositing objects was punishable. I stored objects in places where storing objects was reprehensible. I failed to deliver objects I was legally obligated to deliver. I threw objects out the window of a moving train. I failed to throw litter into litter baskets. I left litter lying in the woods. I threw burning cigarettes into hay. I failed to hand over pamphlets dropped by enemy planes.

I expressed myself by speaking. I expressed myself by appropriating objects. I expressed myself by reproducing live beings. I expressed myself by producing objects. I expressed myself by looking. I expressed myself by playing. I expressed myself by walking.

I walked. I walked purposelessly. I walked purposefully. I walked on paths. I walked on paths on which it was prohibited to walk. I failed to walk on paths when it was imperative to do so. I walked on paths on which it was sinful to walk purposelessly. I walked purposefully when it was imperative to walk purposelessly. I walked on paths on which it was prohibited to walk with an objective. I walked. I walked even when walking was prohibited and against custom. I walked through passages through which it was an act of conformity to pass. I stepped on property on which it was a disgrace to step. I stepped onto property without my identity papers when it was prohibited to step on it without identity papers. I left buildings which it was a lack of solidarity to leave. I entered buildings which it was unseemly to enter without a covered head. I stepped on territory which it was prohibited to step upon. I visited the territory of a state which it was prohibited to visit. I left the territory of a state which it was a hostile act to leave. I drove into streets in a direction it was undisciplined to enter. I walked in directions it was illegal to walk in. I went so far that it was inadvisable to go farther. I stopped when it was impolite to stop. I walked on the right of persons when it was thoughtless to walk on their right. I sat down on seats that were reserved for others to sit on. I failed to walk on when ordered to walk on. I walked slowly when it was imperative to walk quickly. I failed to get on my feet when it was imperative to get on my feet. I lay down in places where it was forbidden to lie down. I stopped at demonstrations. I walked on by when it was imperative to offer help. I entered no-man's-land. I lay down on the floor with R during her

SELF-ACCUSATION

period. I delayed people's flight by walking slowly in narrow hallways. I jumped off moving streetcars. I opened the train door before the train had come to a complete stop.

I spoke. I spoke out. I spoke out what others thought. I only thought what others spoke out. I gave expression to public opinion. I falsified public opinion. I spoke at places where it was impious to speak. I spoke loudly at places where it was inconsiderate to speak loudly. I whispered when it was required to speak up. I remained silent at times when silence was a disgrace. I spoke as a public speaker when it was imperative to speak as a private person. I spoke with persons with whom it was dishonorable to speak. I greeted people whom it was a betrayal of principle to greet. I spoke in a language which it was a hostile act to use. I spoke about objects of which it was tactless to speak. I suppressed my knowledge of a crime. I failed to speak well of the dead. I spoke ill of absent persons. I spoke without being asked to. I spoke to soldiers on duty. I spoke to the driver during the trip.

I failed to observe the rules of the language. I committed linguistic blunders. I used words thoughtlessly. I blindly attributed qualities to the objects in the world. I blindly attributed to the words for the objects words for the qualities of the objects. I regarded the world blindly with the words for the qualities of the objects. I called objects dead. I called complexity lively. I called melancholy black. I called madness bright. I called passion hot. I called anger red. I called the ultimate questions unanswerable. I called the milieu genuine. I called nature free. I called horror frightful. I called laughter liberating. I called freedom inalienable. I called loyalty proverbial. I called fog milky, I called the surface smooth. I called severity Old Testament-like. I called the sinner poor. I called dignity inborn. I called the bomb menacing. I called the doctrine salutary. I called darkness impenetrable. I called morality hypocritical. I called lines of demarcation vague. I called the raised forefinger moralistic. I called mistrust creative. I called trust blind. I called the atmosphere sober. I called conflict productive. I called conclusions futuristic. I called integrity intellectual. I called capitalism corrupt. I called emotions murky. I called the picture of the world distorted. I called the view of the world fuzzy. I called criticism constructive. I called science unbiased. I called precision scientific. I called eyes crystal-clear. I called results easily obtainable. I called the dialogue useful. I called dogma rigid. I called the discussion necessary. I called opinion subjective. I called pathos hollow. I called mysticism obscure. I called thoughts unripe. I called horseplay foolish. I called monotony oppressive. I called solutions obvious. I called being true. I called truth profound. I called lies insipid. I called life rich. I called money of no account. I called reality vulgar. I called the moment delicious. I called war just. I called peace lazy. I called weight dead. I called conflicts irreconcilable. I called the fronts fixed. I called the universe curved. I called snow white. I called ice cold. I called spheres round. I called a something certain. I called the measure full.

I appropriated objects. I acquired objects as property and possessions. I appropriated objects at places where the appropriation of objects was prohibited on principle. I appropriated objects which it was an act hostile to society to appropriate. I claimed objects as private property when it was inopportune to claim I owned them. I declared objects to be public property when it was unethical to remove them from private hands. I treated objects without care when it was prescribed to treat them with care. I touched objects which it was unaesthetic and sinful to touch. I separated objects from objects which it was inadvisable to separate. I failed to keep the required distance from objects from which it was imperative to keep the required distance. I treated persons like objects. I treated animals like persons. I took up contact with living beings with whom it was immoral to take up contact. I touched objects with objects which it was useless to bring into touch with each other. I traded with living beings and objects with which it was inhuman to trade. I treated fragile goods without care. I connected

SELF-ACCUSATION

the positive pole to the positive pole. I used externally applicable medicines internally. I touched exhibited objects. I tore scabs off half-healed wounds. I touched electric wires. I failed to register letters that had to be sent registered. I failed to affix a stamp to applications that required a stamp. I failed to wear mourning clothes upon a death in the family. I failed to use skin cream to protect my skin from the sun. I dealt in slaves. I dealt in uninspected meat. I climbed mountains with shoes unfit for mountain climbing. I failed to wash fresh fruit. I failed to disinfect the clothes of plague victims. I failed to shake the hair lotion before use.

I looked and listened. I looked at. I looked at objects which it was shameless to look at. I failed to look at objects which it was a dereliction of duty to fail to look at. I failed to watch events which it was philistine to fail to watch. I failed to watch events in the position prescribed to watch them. I failed to avert my eyes during events it was treasonable to watch. I looked back when looking back was proof of a bad upbringing. I looked away when it was cowardly to look away. I listened to persons whom it was unprincipaled to listen to. I inspected forbidden areas. I inspected buildings in danger of collapse. I failed to look at persons who were speaking to me. I failed to look at persons with whom I was speaking. I watched unadvisable and objectionable movies. I heard information in the mass media that was hostile to the state. I watched games without a ticket. I stared at strangers. I looked without dark glasses into the sun. I kept my eyes open during sexual intercourse.

I ate. I ate more than I could stomach. I drank more than my bladder could hold. I consumed food and drink. I ingested the four elements. I inhaled and exhaled the four elements. I ate at moments when it was undisciplined to eat. I failed to breathe in the prescribed manner. I breathed air which it was below my station to breathe. I inhaled when it was harmful to inhale. I ate meat during the fast days. I breathed without a gas mask. I ate on the street. I inhaled exhaust gases. I ate without knife and fork. I failed to leave

myself time to breathe. I ate the Host with my teeth. I failed to
breathe through my nose.

I played. I misplayed. I played according to rules which, according
to existing rules, were against convention. I played at times and
places where it was asocial and ingenuous to play. I played with
persons with whom it was dishonorable to play. I played with objects with which it was unceremonious to play. I failed to play at
times and places where it was unsociable to fail to play. I played
according to the rules when it was individualistic not to play according to the rules. I played with myself when it would have been hu-
mane to play with others. I played with powers with whom it was
presumptuous to play. I failed to play seriously. I played too seriously. I played with fire. I played with lighters. I played with marked
cards. I played with human lives. I played with spray cans. I played
with life. I played with feelings. I played myself. I played without chips. I failed to play during playtime. I played with the in-
clination to evil. I played with my thoughts. I played with the
thought of suicide. I played on a thin sheet of ice. I played and
trespassed at one and the same time. I played despair. I played with
my despair. I played with my sex organ. I played with words. I
played with my fingers.

I came into the world afflicted with original sin. My very nature
inclined toward evil. My innate viciousness expressed itself at once
in envy of my fellow suckling. One day in the world, I was no
longer free of sin. Bawling, I craved my mother's breasts. All I
knew was to suck. All I knew was to gratify my desires. With my
reason I refused to recognize the laws that were placed in the
universe and in myself. I was conceived in malice. I was begotten
in malice. I expressed my malice by destroying things. I expressed
my malice by trampling live beings to death. I was disobedient
out of love of play. What I loved in playing was the sense of
winning. I loved in fantastic stories the itch in my ear. I idolized
people. I took greater delight in the trivia of poets than in useful

SELF-ACCUSATION

knowledge. I feared a solecism more than the eternal laws. I let myself be governed solely by my palate. I only trusted my senses. I failed to prove that I had a sense of reality. I not only loved crimes, I loved committing crimes. I preferred to do evil in company. I loved accomplices. I loved complicity. I loved sin for its danger. I did not search for truth. The pleasure I took in art was in my pain and my compassion. I pandered to the desires of my eyes. I failed to recognize the purpose of history. I was godforsaken. I was forsaken by the world. I did not designate the world as *this* world. I also included the heavenly bodies in the world. I was sufficient for myself. I cared only for worldly things. I took no cold bath against melancholy. I took no hot bath against passion. I used my body for wrong ends. I failed to take notice of the facts. I failed to subordinate my physical nature to my spiritual nature. I denied my nature. I ran up against the nature of things. I indiscriminately sought power. I indiscriminately sought money. I failed to teach myself to regard money as a means. I lived in excess of my means. I failed to have the means to put up with the state of affairs. I myself determined how I would fashion my life. I did not overcome myself. I did not toe the line. I disturbed the eternal order. I failed to recognize that evil is only the absence of good. I failed to recognize that evil is only an abuse. I gave birth to death in my sins. I made myself, with my sins, one with the cattle that is to be slaughtered in the slaughterhouse but snuffles at the very iron designed to slaughter it. I failed to resist the beginnings. I failed to find the moment to stop. I made myself an image of the highest being. I sought not to make myself an image of the highest being. I refused to divulge the name of the highest being. I only believed in the three persons of grammar. I told myself that there is no higher being so as not to have to fear it. I looked for the opportunity. I did not use the chance. I did not submit to necessity. I did not count on the possibility. I did not learn from bad examples. I did not learn from the past. I abandoned myself to the free play of forces. I mistook freedom for license. I mistook honesty for self-exposure. I mistook obscenity for originality. I mistook the dream for reality. I mistook life for the cliché. I mistook coercion for necessary guidance. I mistook love for instinct. I mistook the cause for the effect. I failed to observe the unity of thought and action. I failed to see things as they really are. I succumbed to the magic of the moment. I failed to regard existence as a provisional gift. I broke my word. I did not have command of the language. I did not reject the world. I did not affirm authority. I was a naïve believer in authority. I did not husband my sexual powers. I sought lust as an end in itself. I was not sure of myself. I became a puzzle to myself. I wasted my time. I overslept my time. I wanted to stop time. I wanted to speed up time. I was in conflict with time. I did not want to grow older. I did not want to die. I did not let things come toward me. I could not limit myself. I was impatient. I could not wait for it. I did not think of the future. I did not think of *my* future. I lived from one moment to the next. I was domineering. I behaved as though I was alone in the world. I proved ill-bred. I was self-willed. I lacked a will of my own. I did not work on myself. I failed to make work the basis of my existence. I failed to see God in every beggar. I did not eradicate evil at its roots. I irresponsibly thrust children into the world. I failed to adapt my pleasures to my social circumstances. I sought for bad company. I always wanted to be at the center. I was too much alone. I was not enough alone. I led my own life too much. I failed to grasp the meaning of the word "too." I failed to regard the happiness of all mankind as my ultimate aim. I did not place the common interest before the individual interest. I did not face the music. I disregarded orders. I failed to disobey unjustifiable orders. I did not know my limits. I failed to see things in their relationship with one another. I made no virtue of necessity. I switched convictions. I was incorrigible. I failed to put myself at the service of the cause. I was satisfied with the status quo. I saw no one but myself. I yielded to insinuations. I decided neither for one nor for the other. I took no stand. I disturbed the balance of power. I violated generally acknowledged principles. I did not fulfill the quota. I fell behind the goal that had been set. I was one

SELF-ACCUSATION

and everything to myself. I did not take enough fresh air. I woke up too late. I did not clean the sidewalk. I left doors unlocked. I stepped too near the cage. I failed to keep entrances free. I failed to keep exits free. I pulled the safety brake without good reason. I leaned bicycles against forbidden walls. I solicited and peddled. I did not keep the streets clean. I did not take off my shoes. I leaned out the window of a moving train. I handled open fires in rooms that were firetraps. I paid unannounced visits. I did not get up for invalids. I lay down in a hotel bed with a lighted cigarette. I failed to turn off faucets. I spent nights on park benches. I failed to lead dogs on a leash. I failed to muzzle dogs that bit. I failed to leave umbrellas and coats in the cloakroom. I touched goods before I bought them. I failed to close containers immediately after use. I tossed pressurized containers into the fire. I crossed on the red. I walked on superhighways. I walked along the railroad bed. I failed to walk on the sidewalk. I failed to move to the rear in streetcars. I did not hold on to the straps. I used the toilet while the train was stopped in the station. I did not follow personnel instructions. I started motor vehicles where it was prohibited to do so. I failed to push buttons. I crossed the rails in railroad stations. I failed to step back when trains were coming in. I exceeded the load limit in elevators. I disturbed the quiet of the night. I affixed posters to forbidden walls. I tried to open doors by pushing when they could only be pulled open. I tried to open doors by pulling when they could only be pushed open. I roamed the streets after dark. I lit lights during blackouts. I did not remain calm in accidents. I left the house during curfew. I did not stay in my place during catastrophes. I thought of myself first. I indiscriminately rushed out of rooms. I activated alarm signals without authorization. I destroyed alarm signals without authorization. I failed to use emergency exits. I pushed. I trampled. I failed to break the window with the hammer. I blocked the way. I put up unauthorized resistance. I did not stop when challenged. I did not raise my hands above my head. I did not aim at the legs. I played with the trigger of a cocked gun. I failed to save women and children first. I approached the drowning from behind. I kept my hands in my pockets. I took no evasive action. I did not let myself be blindfolded. I did not look for cover. I offered an easy target. I was too slow. I was too fast. I m o v e d.

I did not regard the movement of my shadow as proof of the movement of the earth. I did not regard my fear of the dark as proof of my existence. I did not regard the demands of reason for immortality as proof of life after death. I did not regard my nausea at the thought of the future as proof of my nonexistence after death. I did not regard subsiding pain as proof of the passage of time. I did not regard my lust for life as proof that time stands still.

I am not what I was. I was not what I should have been. I did not become what I should have become. I did not keep what I should have kept.

I went to the theater. I heard this piece. I spoke this piece. I wrote this piece.

KASPAR

1 phase   Can Kaspar, the owner of one sentence, begin and begin to do something with this sentence?

2 phase   Can Kaspar do something against other sentences with his sentence?

3 phase   Can Kaspar at least hold his own against other sentences with his sentence?

4 phase   Can Kaspar defend himself from other sentences and keep quiet even though other sentences prod him to speak?

5 phase   Can Kaspar only become aware of what he speaks through speaking?

6 phase   Can Kaspar, the owner of sentences, do something with these sentences, not only to other sentences but also to the objects of the other sentences?

7 phase   Can Kaspar bring himself into order with sentences about order, or rather, with ordered sentences?

8 phase   Can Kaspar, from the order of a single sentence, derive a whole series of sentences, a series that represents a comprehensive order?

9 phase   Can Kaspar learn what, in each instance, is the model upon which an infinite number of sentences about order can be based?

10 phase   Can Kaspar, with the sentence model he has learned, make the objects accessible to himself or become himself accessible to the objects?

11 phase   Can Kaspar, by means of sentences, make his contribution to the great community of sentences?

12 phase   Can Kaspar be brought to the point where, with rhyming sentences, he will find rhyme and reason in the objects?

KASPAR

13 phase   Can Kaspar put questions to himself?

14 phase   Can Kaspar, with uninhibited sentences which he applies to his old inhibited sentences, reverse the inverted world of these sentences?

15 phase   Can Kaspar defend himself at least with an inverted world of sentences against inverted sentences about the world? Or: Can Kaspar, by inverting inverted sentences, at least avoid the false appearance of rightness?

16 phase   Who is Kaspar now? Kaspar, who is now Kaspar? What is now, Kaspar? What is now Kaspar, Kaspar?

16 YEARS

thixtheen years
thoutheast station
whath thould
whath thould
he do
thoutheast station
thixtheen years
whath thould
the fellow
whath thould
he do
thixtheen years
thoutheast station
what should
he do
the fellow
with hith
thixtheen years

Ernst Jandl

The play *Kaspar* does not show how IT REALLY IS or REALLY WAS with Kaspar Hauser. It shows what IS POSSIBLE with someone. It shows how someone can be made to speak through speaking. The play could also be called *speech torture*. To formalize this torture it is suggested that a kind of magic eye be constructed above the ramp. This eye, without however diverting the audience's attention from the events on stage, indicates, by blinking, the degree of vehemence with which the PROTAGONIST is addressed. The more vehemently he defends himself, the more vehemently he is addressed, the more vehemently the magic eye blinks. (Or one might employ a jerking indicator of the kind used on scales for tests of strength in amusement parks.) Although the sense of what the voices addressing the protagonist say should always be completely comprehensible, their manner of speaking should be that of voices which in reality have a technical medium interposed between themselves and the listeners: telephone voices, radio or television announcers' voices, the voice that tells the time on the phone, the voices of automatic answering services of all kinds, the speech mannerisms of sports commentators, of stadium announcers, of narrators in the more endearing cartoons, of announcers of train arrivals and departures, of interviewers, of gym teachers who by the way they speak make their directions correspond to the sequence of the gymnastic movements, of language course records, of policemen as they speak through bullhorns at demonstrations, etc. etc. These manners of speaking may all be applied to the text, but only in such a way that they clarify the SENSE or NONSENSE of what is being said. The audience need not be aware which manner of speaking is being used at any given moment, but etc. At the same time, the miniature scenes should be projected, enlarged, on the back of the stage.

KASPAR

Kaspar (Kasper means clown in German) does not resemble any other comedian; rather, when he comes on stage he resembles Frankenstein's monster (or King Kong).

The front curtain is already drawn. The audience does not see the stage as a representation of a room that exists somewhere, but as a representation of a stage. The stage represents the stage. On first glance, the objects on the stage look theatrical: not because they imitate other objects, but because the way they are situated with respect to one another does not correspond to their usual arrangement in reality. The objects, although genuine (made of wood, steel, cloth, etc), are instantly recognizable as props. They are play objects. They have no history. The audience cannot imagine that, before they came in and saw the stage, some tale had already taken place on it. At most they can imagine that the stage hands have moved objects hither and thither. Nor should the audience be able to imagine that the props on stage will be part of a play that pretends to take place anywhere except on stage: they should recognize at once that they will witness an event that plays only on stage and not in some other reality. They will not experience a story but watch a theatrical event. This event will last until the curtain comes together at the end of the piece: because no story will take place, the audience will not be in a position to imagine that there is a sequel to the story. The stage should look something like this: the backdrop of the stage consists of a curtain of the same size and fabric as the front curtain. The folds of the curtain are vertical and plentiful, so the audience has difficulty distinguishing the place where the curtain parts. The wings are bare. The props are in front of the backdrop: they are obviously actors' props. They look new, so the audience won't think they are seeing the representation of a junkshop; and to avoid this possibility, the objects are in their normal positions: the chairs are straight up, the broom is leaning, the cushions lie flat, the drawer is where it belongs in the table. However, so the audience won't think it is seeing the representation of a home-furnishing exhibition, the objects are situated without any obvious relationship to each other; they stand there tastelessly, so the audience recognizes a stage in the objects on display. The chairs stand far from the table, as though they had nothing to do with it; they do not stand at the usual angle to the table or at a normal angle toward each other (they should not, however, give a picture of disorder). The table and its drawer face the audience. Elsewhere on stage there is another table, smaller, lower, with only three legs. Center stage is empty. Two chairs stand elsewhere, each with a different backrest, one with a cushion, one without. Somewhere else is a sofa with room for almost five persons. Half the sofa (from the vantage point of those sitting in the center of the auditorium) should be behind the wings, thus indicating backstage. Elsewhere there is a rocking chair. Somewhere else, a broom and shovel, one of them bearing the clearly discernible word STAGE or the name of the theater. Somewhere else, a wastepaper basket with the same inscription. On the large table, but not in the middle, stands a broad-necked bottle with water in it, and next to it a glass. At the back of the stage is a stylish closet with a large key in the lock. None of the props has any particularly unusual characteristic that might puzzle the beholder. In front, in the center of the apron, is a microphone.

The first person in the audience to enter the theater should find the stage lighted softly. Nothing moves on stage. Every theatergoer should have sufficient time to observe each object and grow sick of it or come to want more of it. Finally, the lights are slowly dimmed as usual, an occurrence that might be accompanied by, for example, a continuous muted violin tone ("The tone of the violin is more ample than that of the guitar"—Kaspar). The theater is dark throughout the play. (While the audience comes in and as they wait for the play to begin, this text might be read softly over the microphones, and repeated over and over.)

I
Behind the backdrop, something stirs. The audience detects this in the movement of the curtain. The movement begins on the left or right of the curtain and continues towards the center, gradually becoming more vehement and more rapid. The closer the person behind the curtain comes to the center, the greater the bulge in the curtain. What at first was only a grazing of the curtain becomes, now that the material is obviously pliable, an attempt to break through. The audience realizes more and more clearly that someone wants to get through the curtain onto the stage but has not discovered the slit in the curtain. After several futile tries at the wrong spots—the audience can hear the curtain being thrashed—the person finds the slit that he had not even been looking for. A hand is all one sees at first; the rest of the body slowly follows. The other hand holds on to a hat, so the curtain won't knock it off. With a slight movement, the figure comes on stage, the curtain slipping off it and then falling shut behind it. Kaspar stands on stage.

II
The audience has the opportunity to observe Kaspar's face and makeup: he simply stands there. His makeup is theatrical. For example, he has on a round, wide-brimmed hat with a band; a light-colored shirt with a closed collar; a colorful jacket with many (roughly seven) metal buttons; wide pants; clumsy shoes; on one shoe, for instance, the very long laces have become untied. He looks droll. The colors of his outfit clash with the colors on stage. Only at the second or third glance should the audience realize that his face is a mask; it is a pale color; it is life-like; it may have been fashioned to fit the face of the actor. It expresses astonishment and confusion. The mask-face is round because the expression of astonishment is more theatrical on round, wide faces. Kaspar need not be tall. He stands there and does not move from the spot. He is the incarnation of astonishment.

KASPAR

III

He begins to move. One hand still holds the hat. His way of moving is highly mechanical and artificial. However, he does not move like a puppet. His peculiar way of moving results from his constantly changing from one way of moving to another. For example, he takes the first step with one leg straight out, the other following timorously and "shaking." He might take the next step in the same manner but reverse the order. With the next step, he throws one leg high in the air and drags the other leg heavily behind him; the next step, he has both feet flat on the ground; the next he takes with the wrong foot first, so that with the subsequent step he must put the other leg far forward to catch up with the first leg; he takes the next two steps (his pace quickens and he comes close to toppling over) by placing the right leg on the left and the left leg on the right, and he almost falls; on the next step, he is unable to get one leg past the other and steps on it; again, he barely avoids falling; the next step he takes is so long he almost slips into a split, consequently he must drag the other leg laboriously after him; in the meantime he has tried to move the right leg further forward, but in another direction, so once more he almost loses his balance; on the next step, which is even more hurried, he places one foot toe-forward, the other toe-backwards, whereupon he attempts to align the toe on one foot with the toe on the other, becomes discombobulated, turns on his axis, and, as the audience has feared all along, finally falls to the ground. Before this occurs, however, he has not been walking toward the audience; his walk consists of spirals back and forth across the stage; it is not so much walking as something between an imminent fall and convoluted progress, with one hand holding on to the hat, a hand which remains on his head when he does fall. At the end of his fall, the audience sees Kaspar sitting on the stage floor in something like a disorderly lotus-position. He does not move; only the hand holding the hat becomes autonomous: it gradually lets go of the hat, slips down along his body, dangling awhile before it too stops. Kaspar just sits there.

IV

He begins to speak. He utters a single sentence over and over: I
want to be a person like somebody else was once. *He utters the sentence so that it is obvious that he has no concept of what it means,
without expressing anything but that he lacks awareness of the
meaning of the sentence. He repeats the sentence several times at
regular intervals.*

V

*In the same position on the floor, the lotus position, Kaspar repeats
the sentence, now giving it almost every possible kind of expression.
He utters it with an expression of perseverance, utters it as a question, exclaims it, scans it as though it were verse. He utters it with
an expression of happiness, of relief. He hyphenates the sentence.
He utters it in anger and with impatience; with extreme fear. He
utters it as a greeting, as an invocation in a litany, as an answer to a
question, as an order, as an imprecation. Then, in monotone, he
sings the sentence. Finally he screams it.*

VI

*When this does not get him anywhere, he gets up. First he tries
getting up all at once. He fails. Halfway up, he falls down again. On
the second attempt he gets almost all the way up, only to fall once
more. Now he laboriously draws his legs out from under him, during which process, his toes get caught on the back of his knees. Finally he pries his legs apart with his hands. He stretches out his
legs. He looks at his legs. At the same time he bends his knees,
drawing them toward himself. Suddenly he is squatting. He watches
as the floor leaves him. He points with his hand at the floor which
is becoming more remote. He utters his sentence with an air of
wonderment. Now he is standing upright, turns his head this way
and that, toward the objects on stage, and repeats the sentence:* I
want to be a person like somebody else was once.

KASPAR

VII

He begins to walk again, still in an artificial manner, but now more regularly: for example, the feet are turned inward, the knees stiff; the arms hang slack, as do the fingers. He directs his sentence, not tonelessly yet without expressing anything, at a chair. He directs the sentence, expressing with it that the first chair has not heard him, at the next chair. Walking on, he directs the sentence at the table, expressing with it that neither chair heard him. Still walking, he directs the sentence at the closet, expressing with it that the closet does not hear him. He utters the sentence once more in front of the closet, but without expressing anything: I want to be a person like somebody else was once. *As though by accident, he kicks the closet. Once again he kicks the closet, as though intentionally. He kicks the closet once more: whereupon all the closet doors open, gradually. The audience sees that the closet contains several colorful theatrical costumes. Kaspar does not react to the movement of the closet doors. He has only let himself be pushed back a bit. Now he stands still until the closet doors have stopped moving. He reacts to the open doors with the sentence:* I want to be a person like somebody else was once.

VIII

The tri-sectioning of events now sets in first, Kaspar moves across the stage, now no longer avoiding each object but touching it (and more); second, after having done something to each object, Kaspar says his sentence; third, the prompters now begin to speak from all sides, they make Kaspar speak by speaking. The prompters—three persons, say—remain invisible (their voices are perhaps prerecorded) and speak without undertones or overtones; that is, they speak neither with the usual irony, humor, helpfulness, human warmth, nor with the usual ominousness, dread, incorporeality or supernaturalness: they speak comprehensibly. Over a good amplifying system they speak a text that is not theirs. They do not speak to make sense but to show that they are playing at speaking, and do so with great exertion of their voices even when they speak softly. The following events ensue: the audience sees Kaspar walking from the closet to the sofa and simultaneously hears speaking from all sides.

Kaspar goes to the sofa. He discovers the gaps between the cushions. He puts one hand into a gap. He can't extract his hand. To help extract it, he puts his other hand into the gap. He can't extract either hand. He tugs at the sofa. With one tug he gets both hands free but also flings one sofa cushion onto the floor, whereupon, after a moment of looking, he utters the sentence: I want to be a person like somebody else was once.

Already you have a sentence with which you can make yourself noticeable. With this sentence you can make yourself noticeable in the dark, so no one will think you are an animal. You have a sentence with which you can tell yourself everything that you *can't* tell others. You can explain to yourself how it goes with you. You have a sentence with which you can already contradict the same sentence.

The prompters stop speaking at about the time Kaspar does something to whatever object he happens to be touching: the sofa cushion falls on the floor at the moment the prompters stop speaking; it functions like a period. Kaspar's sentence after each encounter with an object is preceded by a brief pause.

I X

Kaspar walks to the table. He notices the drawer in the table. He tries to turn the knob on the drawer but is unable to. He pulls on the drawer. It comes out a little. He tugs once more at the drawer. The drawer is now askew. He tugs at it once more. The drawer loses hold and falls to the floor. Several objects, such as

The sentence is more useful to you than a word. You can speak a sentence to the end. You can make yourself comfortable with a sentence. You can occupy yourself with a sentence and have gotten several steps further ahead in the meantime. You can make pauses with the sentence. Play off one word against the other. With the

KASPAR

silverware, a box of matches, and coins, fall out of the drawer. After regarding them for a moment Kaspar says: I want to be a person like somebody else was once.

sentence you can compare one word with the other. Only with a sentence, not with a word, can you ask leave to speak.

X

Kaspar walks toward a chair. He tries to walk straight ahead even though the chair is in his way. While walking, he shoves the chair ahead in front of him. Still walking, he becomes entangled in the chair. Still walking, he tries to disentangle himself from the chair. At first he becomes more and more dangerously entwined in it, but then, as he is about to surrender to the chair, he becomes free of it just because he was about to give in. He gives the chair a kick, so that it flies off and falls over. After regarding it for a moment: I want to be a person like somebody else was once.

With the sentence you can pretend to be dumfounded. Assert yourself with the sentence against other sentences. Name everything that comes in your way and move it out of your way. Familiarize yourself with all objects. Make all objects into a sentence with the sentence. You can make all objects into *your* sentence. With this sentence, all objects belong to you. With this sentence, all objects are yours.

XI

Kaspar walks toward the small table. The table has three legs. Kaspar lifts the table with one hand and yanks with the other hand on one leg but is unable to pull it out. He turns the leg, first in the wrong direction. He turns it in the right direction and unscrews the leg. He is still holding the table with the other hand. He slowly withdraws the hand. The table rests on his fingertips. He withdraws his fingertips. The table

To put up resistance. A sentence to divert you. A sentence with which you can tell yourself a story. You have a sentence which gives you something to chew on when you are hungry. A sentence with which you can pretend you are crazy: with which you can go crazy. A sentence to be crazy with: for remaining crazy. You have a sentence with which you can begin to take notice of yourself: with which you can draw attention topples over. *After regarding it for a moment:* I want to be a person like somebody else was once.

away from yourself. A sentence to take a walk with. To stumble over. To come to a halt with in mid-sentence. To count steps with.

XII

Kaspar walks toward the rocking chair. He walks around it. He touches it as though unintentionally. The chair begins to rock, Kaspar takes a step back. The chair continues to rock. Kaspar takes one step farther back. The rocking chair stops moving. Kaspar takes two steps toward the chair and nudges it with his foot, making it move slightly. When the chair is rocking, he uses his hand to make it rock more. When the chair is rocking more strongly, he uses his foot to make it rock even more. When the rocking chair is rocking even more strongly, he gives it an even stronger shove with his hand, so the rocking chair is now rocking dangerously. He gives it one more kick with his foot. Then, as the rocking chair is about to tip over, though it is still not quite certain whether it will fall or go on rocking, he gives it a little shove with his hand which suffices to tip it over. Kaspar runs off from the turned-over chair. Then he returns, step by step. After regarding it for a moment: I want to be a person like somebody else was once.

You have a sentence you can speak from beginning to end and from end to beginning. You have a sentence to say yes and say nay with. You have a sentence to deny with. You have a sentence with which you can make yourself tired or awake. You have a sentence to blindfold yourself with. You have a sentence to bring order into every disorder: with which you can designate every disorder in comparison to another disorder as a comparative order: with which you can declare every disorder an order: can bring yourself into order: can deny every disorder. You have a sentence of which you can make a model for yourself. You have a sentence you can place between yourself and everything else. You are the lucky owner of a sentence which will make every impossible order possible for you and make every possible and real disorder impossible for you: which will exorcise every disorder from you.

KASPAR

XIII

Kaspar takes a look around. A broom is standing there. He walks to the broom. He draws the broom toward himself with his hand or foot, so that it now leans at a wider angle. He tugs once more at the broom, again increasing the angle. Once more, just a little. The broom begins to slip, and falls. After regarding it for a moment: I want to be a person like somebody else was once.

You can no longer imagine anything without the sentence. You are unable to visualize an object without the sentence. Without the sentence, you cannot put one foot in front of the other. You can remember yourself with the sentence because you uttered the sentence while taking your last step, and you can remember the last step you took because you uttered the sentence.

XIV

Kaspar walks toward the one chair that is still upright. He stops in front of it. He remains standing in front of it for the duration of the sentence. Suddenly he sits down. After looking for a moment: I want to be a person like. *He has obviously been interrupted in mid-sentence.*

You can hear yourself. You become aware. You become aware of yourself with the sentence. You become aware of yourself. You come upon something which interrupts the sentence which makes you aware that you have come upon something. You become aware: you can become aware: you are aware.

XV

Kaspar sits there. He is quiet.

You learn to hesitate with the sentence and with the sentence you learn that you are hesitating, and you learn to hear with the sentence and you learn with the sentence that you are hearing, and with the sentence you learn to divide time into time before and time after uttering the sentence, and you learn with the sentence that you are dividing time, just as

you learn with the sentence that
you were elsewhere the last time
you uttered the sentence, just as
you learn with the sentence that
you are elsewhere now, and learn
to speak with the sentence and
learn with the sentence that you
are speaking; and you learn with
the sentence that you are speaking
a sentence, and you learn with the
sentence to speak another
sentence, just as you learn that
there are other sentences, just as
you learn other sentences, and
learn to learn; and you learn with
the sentence that there is an order
and you learn with the sentence to
learn order.

XVI

The stage is blacked out.
You can still crawl off behind the
sentence: hide: contest it. The
sentence can still mean anything.

XVII
*The stage becomes bright. Kaspar
sits there quietly. Nothing
indicates that he is listening. He
is being taught to speak. He would
like to keep his sentence. His
sentence is slowly but surely
exorcised through the speaking of
other sentences. He becomes
confused.*

The sentence doesn't hurt you yet,
not one word. Does hurt you.
Every word does. Hurt, but you
don't know that that which hurts
you is a sentence that. Sentence
hurts you because you don't know
that it is a sentence. Speaking
hurts you but the speaking does
not. Hurt nothing hurts you
because you don't know yet what.
Hurting is everything hurts you
but nothing. Really hurts you the
sentence does. Not hurt you yet
because you don't know yet that it

KASPAR

is. A sentence although you don't know that it is a sentence, it hurts you, because you don't know that it is a sentence that hurts. You.

I want to be a person like somebody else was once.

Kaspar defends himself with his sentence:
I want.
I want to be like once.
I want to be a person like once.
Somebody else.
Like a person else.
Somebody.

He still maintains his sentence:
I want to be a person like somebody else was once.

You begin, with yourself, you, are a, sentence you, could form, of yourself, innumerable, sentences, you sit, there but, you don't, know that, you sit there. You don't sit, there because you, don't know that, you sit there you, can form, a sentence, of yourself, you sit in, your coat, is buttoned, the belt, on your, pants is, too loose, you have, no shoelace you, have no, belt your coat, is unbuttoned, you are not even, there you, are an un, loosed shoe, lace. You cannot defend yourself against any sentence:

He defends himself again:
Was I.
Somebody else like else.
Somebody else a person.
Be like I.
I be I.
Somebody was.
Be one.
I a person.
I want somebody else.
Like somebody else somebody.
Once like somebody.
Was somebody.
Like once.
I want to be somebody like.

The shoelace hurts you. It does not hurt you because it is a shoelace but because you lack the word for it, and the difference between the tight and the loose shoelace hurts you because you don't know the difference between the tight and the loose shoelace. The coat hurts you, and the hair hurts you. You, although you don't hurt yourself, hurt yourself. You hurt yourself because you don't know what is you. The table hurts you, and the curtain hurts you. The words that you hear and the words that you speak hurt you. Nothing hurts you because you don't know what hurting is, and everything hurts,

you don't know what anything
means. Because you don't know
the name of anything, everything
hurts you even if you don't know
that it hurts you because you don't
know what the word hurt means:

The first divergence:
I want to be like somebody else
like somebody else once was
somebody else.

*He resists more vehemently but
with less success:*
One.
Be.
Somebody.
Was.
Want.
Somebody else.

You hear sentences: something
like your sentence: something
comparable. You can play off your
sentence against other sentences
and already accomplish something:
such as becoming used to the open
shoelace. You are becoming used
to other sentences, so that you
cannot do without them any more.
You can no longer imagine your
sentence all alone by its self: it is
no longer your sentence alone: you
are already looking for other
sentences. Something has become
impossible: something else has
become possible:

Somebody else like I like once I
want to be.

*He resists even more vehemently,
but even less successfully:*
Waswant!
Somelike!
Someonce!
SomeI!
Besome!
Likeonce!
Elsh!

Where are you sitting? You are
sitting quietly. What are you
speaking? You are speaking slowly.
What are you breathing? You are
breathing regularly. Where are you
speaking? You are speaking
quickly. What are you breathing?
You are breathing in and out.
When are you sitting? You are
sitting more quietly. Where are

KASPAR

you breathing? You are breathing
more rapidly. When are you
speaking? You are speaking louder.
What are you sitting? You are
breathing. What are you
breathing? You are speaking.
What are you speaking? You are
sitting. Where are you sitting?
You are speaking in and out:

Olce ime kwas askwike lein.

*The prompters address Kaspar very
vehemently:*

Kaspar utters a very long e.

Order. Put. Lie. Sit.

*Kaspar utters an n for not quite as
long a duration as the e.*

Put. Order. Lie. Sit.
Lie. Put. Order. Sit.

Kaspar utters a shorter s.

Sit. Lie. Put. Order.

*Kaspar utters a brief, formally
difficult, r.*

Order. Put. Lie. Sit.

*Kaspar utters a p, and tries to
stretch the p like the other letters,
an endeavor in which he of course
fails utterly.*

Put. Order. Sit. Lie.
Sit. Lie. Order. Stand.

*With great formal difficulties,
Kaspar utters a t.*

Stand. Sit. Lie. Order.

*With great effort, Kaspar utters a
d.*

Lies. Stands. Sits. Completely
ordered:

*Kaspar seeks to produce some kind
of sound by means of movements
such as stomping his feet, scraping,
shoving a chair back and forth,
and finally perhaps by scratching
on his clothes.*

*The prompters are now speaking
calmly, already sure of their
success:*
Hear?
Remain?
Open up?
Hear!
Remain!!
Open up!!!

*Kaspar tries with all his strength to
produce a single sound. He tries it
with his hands and feet. He cannot
do it. His strenuous movements
become weaker and weaker.
Finally he stops moving altogether.
Kaspar has finally been silenced.
His sentence has been exorcised.
Several moments of quiet.*

*The prompters let him mutely
exert himself.*

XVIII
*Kaspar is made to speak. He is
gradually needled into speaking
through the use of speech material.*

The table stands. The table fell
over? The chair fell over! The chair
stands! The chair fell over and
stands? The chair fell over but the
table stands. The table stands or
fell over! Neither the chair fell
over nor the table stands nor the
chair stands nor the table fell
over?! You are sitting on a chair
that fell over:

Kaspar is still mute.

The table is a horror for you. But
the chair is no horror because it is
no table. But your shoelace is a
horror because the broom is no
chair. But the broom is no horror
because it is a table. But the chair
is no horror because it is the table
as well as the shoelace. But the
shoelace is no horror because it is
neither a chair nor a table nor a
broom. But the table is a horror
because it is a table. But the table,
chair, broom, and shoelace are a
horror because they are called
table, chair, broom, and shoelace.
They are a horror to you because
you don't know what they are
called:

KASPAR

Kaspar begins to speak:
Fallen down.
He begins to speak a little:
Because.
Often.
Me.
Never.
Least.
Into.
Let.
Me.
Nothing.
Although.
How.
Because me here at least already.

He comes closer and closer to
uttering a regular sentence:
Into the hands.
Far and wide.
Or there.
Fell out.
Beat eyes.
No is.
Goes neither home.
To the hole.
Goat eyes.
Reservoir.
How dark.
Pronounced dead.
If I myself already here at least
tell.

Eel. Run.
Boiled. From behind.
Right. Later. Horse.
Never stood. Screams.
Faster. Puss. Thrashing.
Whimpers. The knee.
Back. Crawls.
Hut. At once.

They continue to stuff him with
enervating words: For a closet on
which you sit is a chair, or not? Or
a chair on which you sit is a closet
when it stands on the place of the
closet, or not? Or a table which
stands on the place of the
closet is a chair when you sit on it,
or not? Or a chair on which you
sit is a closet as soon as it can be
opened with a key and clothes
hang in it, even if it stands on the
place of the table and you can
sweep the floor with it; or not?

A table is a word you can apply to
the closet, and you have a real
closet and a possible table in
place of the table, and? And a
chair is a word you can apply to
the broom, so that you have a real
broom and a possible chair in place
of the chair, and? And a broom is a
word you can apply to the
shoelace, and you have a real
shoelace and a possible broom in
place of the shoelace, and? And a
shoelace is a word you can apply to
the table, so that you suddenly
have neither a table nor a shoelace
in place of the table, and?

The chair still hurts you, but the
word chair already pleases you.
The table still hurts you but the
word table already pleases you.
The closet still hurts you a little,
but the word closet already pleases
you more. The word shoelace is
beginning to hurt you less because

Candle. Hoarfrost. Stretch.
Awaits. Struggles.
Rats. Unique. Worse.
Walked. Living. Farther.
Jumped. Yes. Should.

Entered am chair without rags on
the shoelace, which meantime
talked to death struck the feet,
without broom on the table, which
are standing turned over some
distance from the closet, barely
two saving drops on the curtain.

the word shoelace pleases you
more and more. The broom hurts
you less the more the word broom
pleases you. Words no longer hurt
you when the word words pleases
you. The sentences please you
more the more the word sentence
pleases you:

Words and things. Chair and
shoelace. Words without things.
Chair without broom. Things
without words. Table without
thing. Closet without shoelace.
Words without table. Neither
words nor things. Neither words
nor shoelace. Neither words nor
table. Table and words. Words
and chair without things. Chair
without shoelace without words
and closet. Words and things.
Things without words. Neither
word nor things. Words and
sentences. Sentences: Sentences:
Sentences:

Kaspar utters a normal sentence:
At that time, while I was still away,
my head never ached as much, and
I was not tortured the way I am
now that I am here.

It becomes dark.

KASPAR

XIX

*It becomes light, Kaspar slowly
begins to speak:*
After I came in, as I see only now,
I put, as I see only now, the sofa
into disorder, whereupon, as I see
only now, the closet door with
which I, as I see only now, played,
as I see only now, with my foot,
was left open, whereupon I, as I
see only now, ripped, as I see only
now, the drawer out of the table,
whereupon, as I see only now, I
threw over another table,
thereupon a rocking chair, as I see
only now, also turned over, as well
as a further chair and broom, as I
see only now, whereupon I walked
toward, as I see only now, the only
chair still standing (as I see only
now) and sat down. I neither saw
anything nor heard anything, and
I felt good. *He gets up.* Now I have
gotten up and noticed at once, not
just now, that my shoelace was
untied. Because I can speak now I
can put the shoelace in order. Ever
since I can speak I can bend down
to the shoelace in normal fashion.
Ever since I can speak I can put
everything in order. *He bends
down toward the shoelace. He
moves one leg forward so as to be
able to bend down better toward
the shoelace. But because he was
standing with the other leg on the
shoelace, he stumbles as he moves
the leg forward and falls after
making a futile attempt to remain
upright—for a moment it looks as*

*though he might stop himself, but
he doesn't. In the process he also
overturns the chair he had been
sitting on. After a moment of
silence:*
Ever since I can speak I can stand
up in a normal fashion; but falling
only hurts ever since I can speak;
but the pain when I fall is half as
bad ever since I know that I can
speak about the pain; but falling is
twice as bad ever since I know that
one can speak about my falling;
but falling doesn't hurt at all any
more ever since I know that I can
forget the pain; but the pain
doesn't stop at all any more ever
since I know that I can feel
ashamed of falling.

x x
Kaspar sets in. He speaks slowly:
Do remember that and don't
forget it!
Do remember that and don't
forget it!
Do remember that and don't
forget it!
Do remember that and don't
forget it!
Do remember that and don't
forget it!
Do remember that and don't
forget it!
Do remember that and don't
forget it!
Do remember that and don't
forget it!
Do remember that and don't
forget it!

Ever since you can speak a normal
sentence you are beginning to
compare everything that you
perceive with this normal sentence,
so that the sentence becomes a
model. Each object you perceive is
that much simpler, the simpler the
sentence with which you can
describe it: that object is a normal
object about which no further
questions remain to be asked after
a short simple sentence: a normal
object is one which is entirely
clarified with a short simple
sentence: all you require for a
normal object is a sentence of
three words: an object is normal
when you don't first have to tell a
story about it. For a normal object

Do remember that and don't
forget it!
Do remember that and don't
forget it!
Do remember that and don't
forget it!

you don't even require a sentence:
for a normal object the word for
the object suffices. Stories only
begin with abnormal objects. You
yourself are normal once you need
to tell no more stories about
yourself: you are normal once your
story is no longer distinguishable
from any other story: when no
thesis about you provokes an
anti-thesis. You should not be able
to hide behind a single sentence
any more. The sentence about
your shoelace and the sentence
about you must be alike except for
one word: in the end they must be
alike to the word.

XXI
*A spotlight follows Kaspar's hand
which is slowly approaching the
loose shoelace. It follows Kaspar's
other hand, which is also
approaching the shoelace. He
slowly crosses one shoelace over
the other. He holds the crossed
ends up. He winds one end
precisely around the other. He
holds up both ends, crossed. He
draws the shoelaces together,
slowly and deliberately. He
elaborately makes a noose with one
lace. He places the other lace
around the noose. He pulls it
through underneath. He draws the
noose tight. The first order has
been created. The spotlight is
extinguished.*

The table stands. With the word
table you think of a table which
stands: a sentence is not needed
any more. The scarf is lying.
When the scarf is lying, something
is not in order. Why is the scarf
lying? The scarf already requires
other sentences. Already the scarf
has a story: does the scarf have a
knot tied at one end, or has
someone thrown the scarf on the
floor? Was the knot ripped off the
scarf? Was someone choked to
death with the scarf? The curtain
is falling just now: at the word
curtain you think of a curtain that
is falling just now: a sentence is
not needed any more. What is
worth striving for is a curtain that
is just falling.

XXII

The spotlight follows Kaspar's hand, which, by pushing up the jacket, approaches the belt, which may be very wide. The spotlight follows Kaspar's other hand, which also moves toward the belt. One hand slips the belt end out of very many belt loops. One hand holds the prong of the buckle while the other draws the belt away from the prong. This hand pulls the belt tight while the other hand puts the prong through the next hole. The belt end, which has become even longer through the tightening of the belt, is again passed carefully through the many loops until the pants fit as they should obviously fit. The spotlight darkens.

A sentence which demands a question is uncomfortable: you cannot feel at ease with such a sentence. What matters is that you form sentences that you can at least feel at ease with. A sentence which demands another sentence is unpretty and uncomfortable. You need homely sentences: sentences as furnishings: sentences which you could actually save: sentences which are a luxury. All objects about which there are still questions to be asked are disorderly, unpretty, and uncomfortable. Every second sentence (*the words are timed to coincide with the loops through which Kaspar is passing the belt*) is disorderly, unpretty, uncomfortable, irksome, ruthless, irresponsible, in bad taste.

XXIII

The spotlight follows Kaspar's hand which is buttoning his jacket from top to bottom. One button is left over at the bottom. The spot points to the leftover button, as does Kaspar's hand. Then it follows the hand as it unbuttons the jacket from bottom to top, but more rapidly than it buttoned it. Then it follows Kaspar's hand as it buttons the jacket once more, even more quickly. This time he succeeds. The spot and Kaspar's

Every object must be the picture of an object: every proper table is the picture of a table. Every house must be the picture of a house. Every proper table is (*the words are timed to coincide with the buttoning*) orderly, pretty, comfortable, peaceful, inconspicuous, useful, in good taste. Each house (*the words coincide with the buttoning*) that tumbles, trembles, smells, burns, is vacant, is haunted is not a true house. Every *hands both point to the bottommost button. Then the hands release the button. The spot reveals that everything is in order. Then it goes out.*

sentence (*the words again coincide with the buttoning*) which doesn't irk, doesn't threaten, doesn't aim, doesn't ask, doesn't choke, doesn't want, doesn't
assert is a
picture of a sentence.

XXIV

The spot shines on Kaspar. It is obvious that his jacket does not match his pants, either in color or in style. Kaspar just stands there.

A table is a true table when the picture of the table coincides with the table: it is not yet a genuine table if the picture of the table alone coincides with the table whereas the picture of the table and chair together do not coincide with the table and chair. The table is not yet a true, actual, genuine, right, correct, orderly, normal, pretty, even prettier, spectacularly beautiful table if you yourself do not fit the table. If the table is already a picture of a table, you cannot change it: if you can't change the table, you must change yourself: you must become a picture of yourself just as you must make the table into a picture of a table and every possible sentence into a picture of a possible sentence.

XXV

Kaspar puts the stage in order. While the spotlight follows him and everything he does, he moves from one object to the other and corrects whatever harm he has done to it. Moreover, he puts the objects into their normal

His actions are accompanied by sentences from the prompters. At first these sentences are adjusted to Kaspar's movements, until Kaspar's movements gradually begin to adjust to the movement of the sentences. The sentences clarify relationships toward each other, so that the stage gradually begins to look inhabitable. Kaspar creates his own (three) walls for himself. Each of his steps and movements is something new to which the spotlight calls attention. Occasionally he accompanies his actions with sentences. Every interruption of the action produces an interruption of the sentence. Every repetition of an action produces a repetition of the sentence. As he nears the completion of his task, his actions more and more obey the sentences of the prompters, whereas in the beginning the prompters' sentences adjusted themselves to his actions. First of all, Kaspar rights the chair on which he had been sitting, saying, for example: I am righting the chair and the chair is standing. *He goes to the second chair and raises it, this time with one hand. The spot shines on the hand, which holds on to a vertical rod on the backrest:* I am putting up the second chair: I can count. The first chair has two rods. The second chair has three rods: I can compare. *He squats down behind the chair and embraces the rods with both hands. He shakes them:* everything that is barred with rods is a chair. *One rod breaks in half. He quickly puts the two halfs together again:* Everything that breaks is only a rod in a chair. Everything that can be covered up

events on the stage, of course without describing them. There is a choice among the following sentences.

Everyone is born with a wealth of talents.

Everyone is responsible for his own progress.

Everything that does harm is made harmless.

Everyone puts himself at the service of the cause. Everyone says yes to himself.

Work develops an awareness of duty in everyone.

Each new order creates disorder.

Everyone feels responsible for the smallest mote of dust on the floor.

Whoever possesses nothing replaces his poverty with work.

All suffering is natural.

Every working man must be given leisure time in accordance with his need to replenish the energy expended while working.

Everyone must build his own world.

Example is a lesson that all men can read.

A foolish consistency is the hobgoblin of little minds.

Good order is the foundation of all things.

KASPAR

is only a rod in a chair. *He walks to the large table. This time, before he kneels down, he pulls his pants up over his knees:* I pull my pants up over my knees so they won't get dirty. *He quickly picks up what had fallen out of the drawer:* Everything that cuts is only a table knife. Everything that lies face up is a playing card. *He tries picking up a match with his whole hand. He fails. He tries with two fingers and succeeds:* Everything I can't pick up with my whole hand is a match. *He quietly pushes the drawer into the table. He still has the match in his hand. He sees another match on the floor. He picks it up, whereupon the match in his hand drops. He picks it up, whereupon the second match falls out of his hand (the movements are very precise, the spot follows). For the first time he uses his other hand to pick up the match. He holds the two matches in his two fists. He no longer has a hand free to open the drawer. He stands before the drawer. Finally he gives the match from one hand to the other hand:* I can hold one hand free. Everything that can move freely is a hand. *He opens the drawer wide, with one hand. He puts the matches in the drawer, pushing the drawer shut with the other hand, whereupon the first hand gets caught in the drawer. He pulls on the caught hand while pushing*

A fanatical desire for order does not have to lead to a coup d'etat.

Every step extends one's perspective.

That table is a meeting place.

The room informs you about its inhabitant.

An apartment is a prerequisite for an orderly life.

Flowers should stand there as though they had a common center.

Don't stand if you can sit.

Bending down expends more energy than anything else.

A burden is lighter the closer it is held to the body.

Put only things you don't use often into the top shelves.

Saving means saving energy.

Balance the weight on both arms.

The table won't run away from you.

Always take a fresh look at your work.

Only if you're healthy can you achieve a lot.

Disorder outrages all decent-thinking men.

One of the most beautiful things in life is a well-set table.

*in with the other hand, exerting
himself more and more in both
endeavors. Finally he is able to free
his hand with one violent pull
while the other hand, with one
violent push, pushes in the drawer.
He does not rub his hand but
moves on immediately, righting the
rocking chair, which had fallen
near the table, almost in one
movement with the bang of the
drawer as it is shut. Immediately
afterward he leans the broom
against the wall. Almost before the
audience has time to realize it, he
is kneeling before the three-legged
table replacing the leg, all his
movements being rapidly followed
by the spotlight. As he moves, he
says, also very rapidly:* Everything
that bangs is only a table drawer:
everything that burns is only a
chapped lip: everything that puts
up resistance is only a fallen
broom: everything that gets in the
way is only a snowdrift: everything
that rocks is only a rocking horse:
everything that dangles is only a
punching ball: everything that
can't move is only a closet door. *In
the meantime he has marched to
the closet door and banged it shut.
But it won't stay shut. He slams it
shut again. It slowly opens again.
He pushes it shut. As soon as he
lets go of it, it opens up again:*
Everything that doesn't close is a
closet door. Everything that
frightens me is only a closet door.
Everything that hits me in the face

The furnishings should
complement you.

Apportion your time correctly.

A place for everything and
everything in its place.

Happy are those who have steered
a middle course.

Nothing is given to you in life.

The fingernails are a special index
of order and cleanliness.

Suggest with a friendly smile that
you like your work.

What has always been the way
you find it, you won't be able to
change at once.

Everyone must be able to do
everything.

Everyone should be completely
absorbed in his work.

Everything that appears to harm
you is only in your best interest.

You should feel responsible for the
furniture.

Sweep the floor in the direction of
the boards.

When you clink glasses, they
should ring clearly.

Every step must become
completely natural to you.

You must be able to
act
independently.

KASPAR

is only a closet door. Everything that bites me is only a closet door. *(Each of these sentences coincides with Kaspar's attempts to slam or push the door shut.) Finally he leaves the closet open. He goes to the sofa, puts it back in order, at the same time shoving it completely on stage. The spotlight precedes him, designating the place where the sofa should stand. Two other spots precede him, showing where the two chairs should stand. He puts the chairs there. (The spotlights are of different colors.) Another spot designates the place for the rocking chair. He follows it and places the rocking chair in its appointed spot. Another light already indicates the place for the little table. He puts it there. Another spot appears, designating the appropriate place for broom and shovel. He wants to put them there but the spot moves on and he follows it. It goes backstage and he follows it there with shovel and broom in hand. The spot returns without him and is already fixed on a place on the stage when Kaspar returns. In his arms he holds a large vase with flowers. He puts the vase in the designated place. Another spot indicates a place on the little table. Kaspar leaves the stage and returns with a plateful of decorative fruit. He puts it on the little table. Another spot designates an empty place in the corner of the stage. He*

Outside show is a poor substitute for
inner worth.

The merit of originality is not novelty; it is sincerity.

The golden rule in life is moderation in all things.

There's nothing in this world constant but inconstancy.

A bad beginning makes a bad ending.

Circumstances are beyond the control of man; but his conduct is in his own hands.

In an orderly room the soul also becomes orderly.

Every object you see for the second time you can already call your own.

The relativeness
of means
is your basic principle.

Running water
does not
become stagnant.

A room
should be
like a picture book.

Sitting all your life
is unhealthy.

A room
should have
a timeless character.

leaves the stage and returns with a small stool. He puts it in its appointed place. Another spot indicates an empty area on the backdrop. He gives a sign to the stage-rigging loft and a painting is lowered onto the empty area. (What the painting represents is of no importance as long as it goes with the furnishings.) Kaspar directs it until it hangs perfectly. He stands there. Another spot walks ahead of him to the open closet. It lights up the clothes. Kaspar goes to the closet. Quickly he takes off his jacket, but finds no place to put it. The spotlight goes backstage and he follows it with the jacket over his arm. He returns with a clothes tree and hangs the jacket up on it. He walks to the closet and picks out another jacket, puts it on, buttons it. He stands there. He takes off his hat. He hangs the hat up on the clothes tree. The stage becomes increasingly more colorful. He has now begun to move in rhythm to the sentences from the prompters. A continuous sound has set in softly. It now becomes louder. It is apparent that the jacket goes with the pants and the other objects. Everything on stage goes with everything else. For a moment Kaspar looks like a dummy at an interior-decoration exhibition. Only the open closet disrupts the harmony of the picture. The continuous tone becomes even

You must show
confidence
in your work.

There are no woodworms
in the door hinges.

You must be able to be proud
of what you have achieved.

Your well-being is determined
by your achievement.

The floor makes a decisive
difference in the overall impression
of the room.

What matters
is to be with it.

Doors lock, but also constitute
connections to the outside world.

The objects
must supplement
your image.

All work is
what you
make of it.

The order
should not be
a soul-less order.

You are
what you have.

Living in a dark room
only brings unnecessary
thoughts.

The order
of the objects
creates
all

KASPAR

louder. Kaspar stands there and lets people look him over. The stage is festively lit.

prerequisites
for
happiness.

What is a nightmare in the dark
is
joyous certainty
in the light.

Every order
eventually looses its
terror.

You're not in the world for fun.

XXVI
The light on stage is very gradually extinguished, the tone adjusting itself to the light. Kaspar is speaking as the light goes out. He begins to speak in a deep, well-modulated voice, but raises it as the light and the continuous sound subside. The darker the stage and the softer the tone, the more shrill and ill-sounding Kaspar's voice becomes. Finally, with the onset of complete darkness and the ceasing of the continuous sound, he is whimpering in the highest registers: Everything that is bright is peaceful: everything that is quiet is peaceful: everything that is in its place is peaceful: everything peaceful is friendly: everything friendly is inhabitable: everything inhabitable is comfortable: everything comfortable is no longer ominous: everything I can

The prompters speak while Kaspar is speaking, however without making him incomprehensible, whereas they themselves are only barely comprehensible because they speak too softly, their words overlap, they leave out syllables, reverse the order of the words, or put the wrong emphasis on them.

name is no longer ominous:
everything that is no longer
ominous belongs to me: I am at
ease with everything that belongs
to me: everything I am at ease
with strengthens my
self-confidence: everything that
belongs to me is familiar to me:
everything I am familiar with
strengthens my self-confidence:
everything that is familiar to me
lets me breathe a sigh of relief:
everything I am familiar with is
orderly: everything that is orderly
is beautiful: everything that is
beautiful is good for my eyes:
everything that is good for my eyes
is good for me: everything that is
good for me makes me good:
everything that makes me good
makes me good for something. *It
is now completely dark. As it again
becomes bright very gradually,
Kaspar begins to speak again, at
first with a pleasant-sounding
voice, but the brighter it becomes,
the higher and shriller his voice
gets:* Everything that is in order is
in order because I say to myself
that it is in order, just as everything
that lies on the floor is a dead fly
because I say to myself that
everything that lies on the floor is
only a dead fly, just as everything
that lies on the floor lies there only
for a short while because I say to
myself that it lies there only for a
short while, just as everything that
lies gets up again because I say to
myself that it gets up again, just as

*In regular sequence they speak
something like the following text:*
Hit the table. Sat between the
chairs. Rolled up the sleeves.
Stayed on the floor. Looked behind
curtains. Spat into hands. Struck
the table. Stayed on the floor.
Rolled up sleeves. Sat down
between chairs. Sat down at the
table together. Struck the table. Sat
down in the nettles. Slammed the
door. Rolled up sleeves. Struck the
chairs. Beaten to a pulp. Struck the
table. Sat down in the nettles.
Knocked down. Spit in front of
feet. Struck between the eyes.
Broke the china. Stayed tough. Sat
down in the nettles. Knocked out.
Beat down the request. Showed
the fists. Beaten to a pulp. Struck
a low blow. Exterminated from
head to toe. Smashed the floor.
Spat in front of the feet. Struck
between the eyes. Broke the china.
Pushed into the nettles. Smashed
the table. Struck a low blow.
Smashed the communal table.
Struck down. Smashed the set.
Smashed the door. Struck down
the heckler. Stayed tough.
Smashed all prejudices.

KASPAR

everything that I say to myself is in order because I say to myself that everything that I say to myself is in order.

XXVII

Kaspar is now taught the model sentences with which an orderly person struggles through life. While he was uttering his last sentences, he sat down in the rocking chair. During the following course of instruction he continues to sit in the chair, but begins to rock only gradually. At first he drawls his words, although speaking with intensity, without punctuation marks; then he begins to speak with full stops, finally with hyphens, finally he makes exaggerated sense, and ultimately he utters model sentences.

While Kaspar is sitting in the rocking chair, the words the prompters uttered just now, which anticipate the aphorisms, are repeated: now, because Kaspar is silent, they are more comprehensible and become completely comprehensible toward the end, and then turn into the following model sentences: Every sentence helps you along: you get over every object with a sentence: a sentence helps you get over an object when you can't really get over it, so that you really get over it: a sentence helps you to get over every other sentence by letting itself take the place of the other sentence: the door has two sides: truth has two sides: if the door had three sides, truth would have three sides: the door has many sides: truth has many sides: the door: the truth: no truth without a door. You beat the dust off your pants: you beat the thought out of your head: if you couldn't beat the dust off your pants, you couldn't beat the thought out of your head. You finish speaking: you finish thinking: if you couldn't finish speaking, you couldn't say the sentence: I finish thinking. You look again: you think again: if you couldn't look again, you couldn't say the sentence: I reflect: if you couldn't look again, you couldn't reflect.

The pupil of the eye is round fear is round had the pupil perished fear would have perished but the pupil is there and fear is there if the pupil weren't honest I couldn't say fear is honest if the pupil were not permitted fear wouldn't be permitted no fear without pupil if the pupil weren't moderate I couldn't say fear only arises at room temperature fear is less honest than is permitted fear is drenched warm as a hand on the contrary

You are standing. The table is standing. The table is not standing, it was placed there. You are lying. The corpse is lying. The corpse is not lying, it was placed there. If you couldn't stand and if you couldn't lie, you couldn't say: the table is standing, and the corpse is lying: if you couldn't lie and stand, you couldn't say: I can neither lie nor stand.

A fat man is true to life cold sweat is commonplace if a fat man weren't true to life and if his cold sweat weren't commonplace a fat man couldn't become afraid and if a fat man couldn't lie on his stomach I couldn't say he neither stands up nor can he sing

The room is small but mine. The stool is low but comfortable. The sentence is harsh but just. The

KASPAR

rich man is rich but friendly. The
poor man is poor but happy. The
old man is old but sturdy. The star
is famous but modest. The
madman is mad but harmless. The
criminal is scum but a human
being nonetheless. The cripple is
pitiable but also a human being.
The stranger is different, but it
doesn't matter:

But the snow falls contentedly.
The fly runs over the water but not
excessively. The soldier crawls
through the mud but pleasurably.
The whip cracks on the back but
aware of its limits. The fool runs
into the trap but at peace with the
world. The condemned man leaps
into the air but judiciously. The
factory gate squeaks but that
passes away.

The ring is decorative as well as an
object of value. The community
is not only a burden but also a joy.
War is indeed a misfortune, but
sometimes inescapable. The future
is obscure but it also belongs to
the enterprising. Playing is not
only a diversion, but is also a
preparation for reality. Force is
indeed a dubious method, but it
can be useful. A harsh youth is
indeed unjust, but it makes you
hard. Hunger is bad indeed, but
there are worse things. Whipping
is reprehensible indeed, but one
also has to see the positive side:

The sunflowers are not only
abundant, but also summer and
winter. The corners are glowing

indeed, but for dying of thirst they
are not only made to order but
also spend a meditative old age
observed by daylight. The better
solutions are not only not worth
striving for, but indeed eat right
out of my hand, yet will also
decisively and emphatically reject
any and all interference.

The more lovingly the table has
been laid, the more you love to
come home. The greater the want
of space, the more dangerous the
thoughts. The more happily you
work, the more quickly you find a
way to yourself. The more
self-assured you are, the easier it is
for you to get ahead. The greater
the mutual trust, the more
bearable the living together. The
more the hand perspires, the less
sure of himself the man is. The
cleaner the apartment, the cleaner
the tenant. The farther south you
go, the lazier the people:

The more wood on the roof, the
more mildew in the bread oven.
The more cities with cellars, the
more machinations on the slag
heaps. The brighter the
clotheslines, the more suicides in
the trade department. The more
emphatic the demand for reason
in the mountains, the more
ingratiating the dog-eat-dog laws
of free nature.

It goes without saying that a large
vase stands on the floor, just as it
goes without saying that a smaller
vase stands on a stool, while it goes

KASPAR

without saying that an even smaller vase stands on a chair, just as it goes without saying that an even smaller vase stands on the table, while it goes without saying that creepers stand even higher. It goes without saying that well-being is determined by achievement. It goes without saying that despair is out of place here:

It goes without saying that the flour sack strikes the rat dead. It goes without saying that hot bread lets children come prematurely into the world. It goes without saying that discarded matches introduce a demonstration of confidence.

You gain something new from each object. No one stands on the sidelines. Every day the sun rises. No one is irreplaceable. Every new building means peace. No one is an island. Every industrious person is liked everywhere. No one is allowed to shirk his task. Each new shoe hurts in the beginning. No one has the right to exploit another. Every courteous person is punctual. No one who has a high opinion of himself lets others do his work for him. Every sensible person will bear the whole situation in mind with every step he takes. No one points the finger at others. Every person deserves respect, even a cleaning woman.

Every split straw is a vote for the progressive forces. No country fair means security for all. Each dripping faucet is an example of a healthy life. No sensible arm is lifted for the burning department store. Every pneumatic-drill operator who comes upon a corpse corresponds to a rapid-firing mechanism that can deliver six thousand rounds per minute.

A cat is no getting on. A stone is not a completely satisfied need. A strawman is no body count. Running away is no equality of rights. To stretch a rope across the path is no permanent value.

Poverty is no disgrace. War is not a game. A state is not a gangster organization. An apartment is no sanctuary. Work is no picnic. Freedom is no license. Silence is no excuse. A conversation is no interrogation.

The appendix bursts. The grenade bursts. If the appendix couldn't burst, you couldn't say: the grenade bursts.

The dog barks. The commander barks.

The water is rising. The fever is rising. If the water couldn't rise, the fever couldn't rise.

The avalanche roars. The angry man roars.

The angry man thunders. Thunder thunders. Without the angry man, thunder couldn't thunder.

The flags flutter. The eyelids flutter.

The balloon swells. The jubilation swells. Without the balloon, the jubilation couldn't swell.

The laughing man gurgles. The swamp gurgles.

The nervous nelly jerks. The hanged man jerks. If it weren't for the nervous nelly, the hanged man couldn't jerk.

KASPAR

The firewood cracks. The bones
crack.

The blood screams to high heaven.
The injustice screams to high
heaven. Without the blood,
injustice could not scream to high
heaven.

The door springs open. The skin
springs open. The match burns.
The slap burns. The grass
trembles. The fearful girl trembles.
The slap in the face smacks. The
body smacks. The tongue licks.
The flame licks. The saw screeches.
The torture victim screeches. The
lark trills. The policeman trills.
The blood stops. The breath stops.

It is not true that the conditions
are as they are represented; on the
contrary, it is true that the
conditions are different from their
representation.

It is untrue that the representation
of the conditions is the only
possible representation of the
conditions: on the contrary, it is
true that there exist other
possibilities of the representation
of the conditions. *Kaspar speaks
along with the prompters to the
end of this sequence.*

It is untrue that the representation
of the conditions is the only
possible representation of the
conditions: on the contrary, it is
true that there exist other
possibilities of the representation
of the conditions. It does not
correspond to the facts to
represent the conditions at all; on
the contrary, it corresponds to the
facts not to represent them at all.
That the conditions correspond to
the facts is untrue.

You bend down; someone sees you
you rise; you see yourself. You

move yourself; someone reminds you; you set yourself down; you remember yourself. You are afraid of yourself; someone quiets you; someone explains you; you rush yourself; you explain yourself; you disquiet yourself:

I am quieting myself.

You were already making a fist.

I was still screaming.

You still took a deep breath.

I was already there.

The chair still stands in its place.

I was still standing.

Nothing has changed yet.

I was already awake.

The door is already shut tight.

I was already kicking.

Some were still sleeping.

I am whispering already.

One can still hear throbbing.

I still wasn't hearing anything.

Some still won't listen.

I am outside already.

Here and there someone is still moving.

I am still unbelieving.

Many are already placing their hands on the head.

I am already running.

KASPAR

I am pulling in my head already.

I am already hearing.

I already understand.

I know already.

went past

living weight

light and easy

within reach

nothing to look for

a better life

good laugh

master everything

will win everywhere

Some are still breathing.

Someone still objected.

A single person is still whispering.

Single shots are still being fired.

you

you

you

you

you

you

you

you

you

you

lowered the mother mortality

        you

was leading

        you

more and more comprehensively

        you

free of

        you

is peace and future

        you

a relationship to the world

        you

which moved things closer

        you

peaceful purposes

        you

constantly growing

        you

in case of emergency to

        you

only for protection

        you

irresistibly

        you

stretched myself

        you

trampled

KASPAR

called

was and is

recognized me.

you

you

you

You know what you are saying.
You say what you are thinking.
You think like you feel. You feel
what it depends on.

You know on what it depends.
You know what you want. You can
if you want to. You can if you only
want to. You can if you must.

You only want what everyone
wants. You want because you feel
pressed. You feel you can do it.
You must because you can.

Say what you think. You can't say
except what you think. You can't
say anything except what you are
also thinking. Say what you think.
When you want to say what you
don't think you must begin to
think it that very moment. Say
what you think. You can begin to
speak. You must begin to speak.
When you begin to speak you will
begin to think what you speak
even when you want to think
something different. Say what you
think. Say what you don't think.
When you have begun to speak
you will think what you are saying.
You think what you are saying,
that means you can think what

you are saying, that means it is
good that you think what you are
saying, that means you ought to
think what you are saying, that
means, on the one hand, that you
may think what you are saying,
and on the other hand, that you
must think what you are saying,
because you are not allowed to
think anything *different* from what
you are saying. Think what you are
saying:

When I am, I was. When I was, I
am. When I am, I will be. When I
will be, I was. Although I was, I
will be. Although I will be, I am.
As often as I am, I have been. As
often as I have been, I was. While
I was, I have been. While I have
been, I will be. Since I will be, I
will have been. Since I have been,
I am. Due to the fact that I am, I
have been. Due to the fact that
I have been, I was. Without
having been, I was. Without
having been, I will be. So that I
will be, I have been. So that I will
have been, I have been. Before I
was, I was. Before I had become,
I am. I am so that I will have
become. I will have become so
that I was. I was as soon as I will
have become. I will have become
as soon as I will be. I will be while
I will have become. I will have
become while I had become. I
became because I will have
become. I will have become
because I became. I became
because I will have become. I will

have become because I am.
I am the one I am.
I am the one I am.
I am the one I am.

Kaspar stops rocking.

Why are there so many black
worms flying about?

The stage becomes black.

XXVIII

*As it grows light again after several
moments of quiet, the prompters
speak once more:* You have model
sentences with which you can get
through life: by applying these
models to your sentences, you can
impose order on everything that
appears chaotic: you can declare it
ordered: every object can be what
you designate it to be: if you *see*
the object differently from the way
you *speak* of it, you must be
mistaken: you must say to yourself
that you are mistaken and you *will*
see the object: if you don't *want* to
say that to yourself, then it is
obvious that you want to be
forced, and thus do want to say it
in the end.

*It has now become very bright.
Kaspar is quiet.*

XXIX

You can learn and make yourself
useful. Even if there are no limits:
you can draw them. You can
perceive: notice: become aware in

all innocence: every object
becomes a valuable. You can
develop in an orderly fashion.

*It becomes even brighter: Kaspar
is even quieter.*

XXX

You can quiet yourself with
sentences: you can be nice and
quiet.

*It is very bright. Kaspar is very
quiet.*

XXXI

You've been cracked open.

XXXII

*The stage becomes dark suddenly.
After a moment:* You become
sensitive to dirt.

XXXIII
*It becomes bright, but not very.
Kaspar is sitting in the rocking
chair. A second Kaspar with the
same kind of face-like mask, the
same costume, comes on stage
from the wings. He enters,
sweeping with a broom. He quickly
cleans the stage, each movement
being made distinctly visible, for
example, by the spot. In passing he
gives the closet door a shove, but it
won't stay shut. He cleans carefully
under the sofa. He sweeps the dirt
into a pile at the edge on the side
of the stage. He walks across the*

*stage to fetch the shovel. He walks
back to the pile of dirt and sweeps
the dirt onto the shovel. He does
not succeed in sweeping the dirt
onto the shovel with a single swipe
of the broom, nor quite with the
second swipe. By zigzagging
backwards across the stage,
between objects, without however
bothering the first Kaspar, he
continues to try to sweep the rest
of the dirt onto the shovel. He
sweeps and sweeps until he
disappears backstage. At that
moment the stage darkens.*

XXXIV

After a moment: Become aware
that you are moving.

XXXV
*It becomes bright. A third Kaspar
appears on stage from the wings,
accompanying a fourth Kaspar,
who walks on crutches, dragging
his legs, moving very very slowly,
almost imperceptibly. The third
Kaspar repeatedly increases his
pace somewhat, but each time has
to wait for the fourth Kaspar to
catch up with him. That takes
time. They walk across stage front,
Kaspar 3 nearer to the audience
than Kaspar 4. Kaspar 3 to some
extent adopts the gait of Kaspar 4,
but in part retains his own manner
of walking and therefore still has
to wait for Kaspar 4 to catch up
with him. So both are lurching, as
they say, almost "unbearably"*

slowly across the stage, past Kaspar
1. When they have finally gone,
the stage darkens instantly.

XXXVI

After a moment: What you can't
deal with, you can play with.

XXXVII
It becomes bright. Two further
Kaspars come toward each other
across the stage from different
directions. They want to get past
each other. Both step aside in the
same direction, and bump into
each other. They step aside in the
other direction, and bump into
each other again. They repeat the
attempt in the first direction, and
almost bump into each other.
What looked awkward and
unnatural at first gradually
assumes a rhythm. The
movements become more
rapid and also more regular. The
two Kaspars no longer walk into
each other. Finally they move only
the upper part of their body, then
only their heads jerk, and finally
they stand still. The next moment
they make a wide, elegant curve
around each other and walk off
stage to the left and right.
During these attempts at
circumnavigation, Kaspar 1 has
tried to fold an unfolded road
map. He does not succeed. Finally
he begins playing with the map, as
though it were an accordion, say.
Suddenly the map lets itself be
folded thus, and that is the

KASPAR

*moment when the other Kaspars
leave the stage and it darkens.*

XXXVIII

After a moment: To become aware
that everything falls back into
order of its own accord.

XXXIX
*It becomes bright. Another Kaspar
steps out of the wings. He steps in
front of the sofa, on which there is
a thick cushion. He pushes
with one fist into the cushion and
steps aside. The audience sees the
cushion slowly regain its original
shape. This can also be projected
on the backdrop. With a final tiny
jolt, the cushion regains its original
form. The stage darkens at once.*

XL

After a moment: Movements.

XLI
*Another Kaspar steps on stage. He
has a ball in one hand. He places
the ball on the floor and steps
back. The ball rolls off. Kaspar 1
puts the ball where it was first. The
ball rolls off. Kaspar holds his hand
on the ball for a considerable
period of time. He steps back. The
ball rolls off. The stage darkens.*

XLII

After a moment: Pains.

XLIII
*It is still dark; the audience sees
two matches being lit on stage.
When it grows bright again,
Kaspar 1 is sitting in the rocking
chair, the other Kaspar on the sofa.
Each is holding a burning match
between his fingers. The flames
touch the fingers. Neither Kaspar
emits a sound. The stage darkens.*

XLIV

After a moment: Sounds.

XLV
*As it becomes bright, Kaspar 1 is
alone on stage, standing by the
large table. He takes the
broad-necked bottle and pours a
little water into the glass standing
next to the bottle. The sound of
pouring water is distinctly audible.
He stops pouring. Quickly he
pours the water from the glass back
into the bottle. He takes the bottle
and pours water slowly into the
glass. The sound of pouring water
is even more distinct. When the
glass is full, the stage darkens.*

XLVI

After a moment: A tone.

XLVII
*When it becomes bright, even
more quickly than before, another
Kaspar is standing at the side of*

*the stage while Kaspar 1 is standing
by the table. He is holding a thick
roll of paper which is held together
by a rubber band. Slowly but surely
he forces the rubber band off the
roll. The band snaps off, a tone is
heard. At once the stage darkens.*

XLVIII

After a moment: A view.

XLIX
*The audience hears a noise while
the stage is still dark. When it
becomes bright, Kaspar 1 is again
alone on the stage, sitting by the
table with the plastic fruit on it.
He is holding a partially peeled
apple in his hand. He continues
peeling, the peel growing longer
and longer, and stops peeling
shortly before the apple has been
completely peeled. He places the
apple on top of the decorative
fruit. The peel hangs way down.
The stage darkens.*

L

The prompters remain silent.

LI
*It becomes bright. Kaspar is standing in the center of the stage, be-
tween the table and the closet. With one hand he is forcibly open-
ing the other hand, which is a fist, finger by finger. The fist resists
more and more tenaciously. Finally he wrenches open the hand. It
is empty. The stage darkens.*

LII
*It quickly becomes bright. Another Kaspar is sitting on the sofa.
Kaspar sees the other Kaspar. The stage darkens.*

LIII
*It becomes bright even more quickly. Kaspar is again alone on the
stage, standing in front of the closet, his face to the audience. The
stage darkens.*

LIV
*It becomes bright more quickly still. Kaspar looks down at himself.
The stage darkens.*

LV
*Kaspar tries to catch himself. First he runs in a wide circle across the
stage, then in smaller circles, spiraling in on himself until he turns
on the same spot. He reaches for himself but, because he is standing on one spot, only seizes himself with his own arms . . . whereupon he becomes still and the stage darkens.*

LVI
*It becomes bright more quickly still. Kaspar is standing in front
of the closet, his back to the audience. It darkens.*

LVII
*It becomes bright. Kaspar is in the process of closing the closet
doors. He presses on them for some time. He steps back. The doors
stay shut. The stage darkens.*

LVIII
*It becomes bright. It is very bright. Kaspar leans back against the
closet. The stage looks harmonious. A chord. A spotlight is trained
on Kaspar. He assumes various poses. He continues to alter the*

KASPAR

position of his arms and legs. Say, his arms are akimbo, he shoves
one leg forward, lets his arms drop, crosses his legs, puts his hands in
his pockets, first in his pants pockets, then in his jacket pockets,
stands there with his legs apart, finally crosses his hands over his
stomach, puts his feet close together, finally his arms are akimbo
again. His legs are still close together. He begins to speak:
I am healthy and strong. I am honest and frugal. I am conscientious.
I am industrious, reticent and modest. I am always friendly. I make
no great demands. My ways are winning and natural. Everyone
likes me. I can deal with everything. I am here for everyone. My
love of order and cleanliness has never given reason for complaint.
My knowledge is above average. Everything I am asked to do, I do
perfectly. Anyone can provide the desired information about me. I
am peace-loving and have an untarnished record. I am not one of
those who start a big hue and cry over every little thing. I am calm,
dutiful, and receptive. I can become enthusiastic about every worthy
cause. I would like to get ahead. I would like to learn. I would like
to be useful. I have a concept of length, height, and breadth. I
know what matters. I treat objects with feeling. I have already become used to everything. I am better. I am well. I am ready to die.
My head feels light. I can finally be left alone. I would like to put
my best foot forward. I don't accuse anyone. I laugh a lot. I can
make head and tails of everything. I have no unusual characteristics.
I don't show my upper gums when I laugh. I have no scar under
the right eye and no birthmark under the left ear. I am no public
menace. I would like to be a member. I would like to cooperate. I
am proud of what has been achieved so far. I am taken care of for
the moment. I am prepared to be interrogated. A new part of my life
lies ahead of me. That is my right hand, that is my left hand. If
worst comes to worst, I can hide under the furniture. It was always
my wish to be with it.
He pulls away from the closet, takes two or three steps, the closet
stays shut:
At one time I may have felt as though I didn't even exist; now I
feel as though I exist too much, and the objects, of which there

were too many at one time, now have become almost too few for me.

In the meantime he has walked farther forward. The closet stays shut:

Once plagued by sentences
I now can't have enough of sentences.
Once haunted by words
I now play with every single letter.

He remains standing in the same spot:

At one time I only spoke when asked,
now I speak of my own accord, but now
I can wait to speak until I am asked.

He takes one or two steps more:

Earlier on, each rational sentence was a burden to me
and I detested each rational order
but from now on
I will be rational.

He either does or does not take a step:

Earlier, I threw down one chair, then a second, and then a third:
now, with the introduction of order, my habits are changing.

He takes roughly one step:

I am quiet
now I do not want
to be someone else any more
nothing incites me
against myself any more.
Every object
has become
accessible
to me
and I
am receptive
to each object.
Now I know what I want:
I want

KASPAR

to be
quiet
and every object
that I find sinister
I designate as mine
so that it stops
being sinister to me.

He walks off to the side of the stage but returns after several steps, as though he still had something more to say. He says nothing. He leaves again, taking more steps than the last time, but again steps halfway back onto the stage, as though he had something left to say. He says nothing. He almost leaves, but takes one or two steps back, again as though he had something left to say. He says nothing. Then he departs rapidly. On the now uninhabited stage the closet doors gradually open. When the wide-open closet doors have come to a complete rest, the stage darkens at a stroke, at the same time the auditorium becomes bright. It is intermission. The auditorium doors are opened.

LIX

After a few moments the INTERMISSION TEXT *is piped through loudspeakers into the auditorium, into the lobbies, and even out onto the street if that is possible. At first these texts are quite low and barely audible. The texts consist of tapes of the prompters' speeches, sheer noise, actual taped speeches by party leaders, popes, public speakers of every kind, presidents and prime ministers, perhaps even statements by writers and poets speaking at official functions. The sentences should never be complete, but should be complemented and superseded by other mangled sentences. Although the audience should not be kept from entering into well-deserved conversation, its relaxed mood ought to be disturbed now and then by the intermission texts. Some members of the audience might even be able to listen with one ear while devoting themselves to their drinks. The text might be as follows: (Noises, such as the clinking of glasses.)* free of all worries of the present, we will have the last word. The surplus is lower than the criterion which has been anticipated. (*Louder clinking of glasses.*) What once was not an incalculable demand now becomes much too unexpected for many, and much too early. We need more courage if we can't be saved. A new mass flight south is more important than a murder that never occurred. It is often unjustly forgotten how healthy it is to be a Marine. We want to work to the last man. Don't think of what your country can do for you but climb up the wall. (*The sound of a large truck approaching, then disappearing.*) Criticism helps all real progress no matter the deposits in the glands. Animal herds should beware of the clear mountain air. The results exist to be burned without compunction. Without a certain number of dead each week, it neither goes upward nor downward. Hunger helps no one and doesn't teach anyone manners. (*Meanwhile, the blades of a large rotary saw have begun to clatter. This sound becomes increasingly louder.*) In recent times the voices have increased that have great difficulty playing with themselves. The sides of the scale of justice lower themselves toward each other at the end although everyone is prepared to make sacrifices. With respect to the rat plague we must reach a mutually satisfactory result. Everyone should finally open his ears and listen to the truth when the brand name is announced. What now matters most is to objectively examine the whole realm of concepts associated with each demand. No one can depend on the fact that dooms the situation. (*The saw blades penetrate wood with a screech; however, the noise soon turns into that of a gentle waterfall.*) Nothing that comes from the outside is a distorted picture simply for that and no other simple reason. The human element appears quite ineradicable. We always exist under the condition that we refuse to let irresponsible circles rob us of the view of the public nuisance which is the world. Every declaration of war is designed for each case of patience which has been exhausted. Convincing someone in the nicest possible manner does not have to end with a blow of the water level on the head. Everyone is called upon to the extent of calling the thing by its well-deserved name. The police always has a time of it because it must justify itself. None of us is entirely innocent of the time of day. (*Whistling, booing, stomping, the sound of waves.*) A skeptical stock market gets off best. At least we don't want the employees to have to pay extra even though many things speak for breaking it off. Impudence itself is no silver star. Of course the refugees have to be helped but running away with bare feet is not one of our problems. We know how to handle the glasses more and more. Uniformed persons know the difficulties when it suddenly becomes dark. The robes of the judges are breathtaking when all that is at stake is the shabby whole. We all want to move with profound seriousness which is what matters. (*A swelling football cheer which breaks off with a profound sigh, then a resurgence of it which turns into regularly increasing and decreasing cheers.*) Griping is easier than finding oneself a well-deserved apartment. We'll inflict injuries on the head and chest of anyone who is of the same opinion as we are. The right of hospitality not only cannot be superseded as a concept but one must point to it if necessary with a brain stroke. A screwdriver in the windpipe is appropriate remuneration for someone who never did anything but someone else's duty. Anyone who considers himself someone loses his nerve when angling. We'll accept anyone into the bargain who shakes the foundations. (*A sharply braking car; simultaneously, a jet of water from a firehose.*) The transformation of society into any number of possible mass demonstrations corresponds to a pacifier for a blind man. The war in the sandbox has cost many a live corpse. Anyone who thinks the way he acts only strengthens the neck of the one who thinks differently. No one deserves a fate that makes him level with the ground. Life used to be more worthwhile at one time but now it is no brushfire any more. (*Long-drawn-out factory siren or foghorn.*) What was said of the property owners matters even less with respect to the flesh wounds. Anyone who kills in blind fury fools himself to an extent that is questionable in the least. Anyone who protests against the delivery of goods must also protest against revisionist thinking. We value the strength of a freely reached decision more than sharks chasing swimmers.

Self-assurance contributes a great deal toward continuing useful conversations. Too little has been said so far about the minorities who proudly crawl off into their corners. (*The scraping of chairs on a stone floor.*) What was once forbidden has now been outlawed. Every outward order enables a peaceful and measured exchange of ideas. We regard the either/or as the mark of a free man. We all have to make an effort to be understanding when a dead man assumes the color of grass. A murder does not necessarily have to be equated with a nose dive. A third-degree burn clogs every gasoline line. (*Sounds of horses' hoofs, together with the sound of seats being turned up, street noises, doors being slammed shut, typewriter noises.*) No one is beaten until he is ripe for retirement without good reason. The right to own estates requires no elaborate justification. A loosening-up exercise corresponds to the length of a nightstick between two legs. Whereas every suicide used to be left-handed, the regulation has now become uniform. No lull in the fighting permits time to count the sleeping flies on the ceiling of the cowshed. A single person perched on the church steeple can be equated with an incitement to riot. If one confronts a violent person by oneself, one is oneself a violent person, whereas when one confronts a violent person in the company of six or four men, thereupon the former becomes gentle of his own accord and is gentle. (*Even before this last sentence, the sounds have changed and become distorted musical noises, as if a record is being played at inordinately slow speed; a monotonous, rhythmic music should be utilized for this purpose. In between a faucet is gradually turned on to full strength, then the stopper in a bathtub is pulled out; in addition there may be heavy breathing noises, then the sound of whiplashes, sudden bursts of laughter as after a joke, women's laughter as if at a cocktail party. While all this is going on, the audience should be able to hear, although not quite comprehending, the spoken text. Then follows a short moment of quiet, then noise once again and the reading of texts, then a longer moment of quiet, then something like the following text by itself.*) A beautifully laid table. Everything in the best order. You're in no great hurry. You help your companion take off the coat. The colorful tablecloth delights everyone. The knife lies on the right. The napkin on the left. The plate stands in the middle. The cup stands at the right and to the back. The knife lies in front of the cup. The towel hangs to the right of the knife. Your finger rests on the towel. To the right of the towel is the first-aid kit. The plates are handed from the left. The soup is handed from the right. The drinks are handed from the right. Everything that you serve yourself is handed from the left. The stab comes from the right. You are sitting in the middle. The salt shaker stands on the left. The spoon is lying on the outside to the right of the knife. The spoon lies bottom up. The grip that chokes comes from both sides. Your hand is lying on the table. The edge of the knife is facing left. As seen from your seat, the heart of the person opposite you is on the right. The glass stands to the right of the plate. You drink in small sips. The blow is more effective when it comes from below. The bouquet of flowers is in the center of the table. The fork lies to the left of the plate. You can't give white flowers to the dying. You sit upright on principle. The older one is on the right. The bouquet does not block your view of the person opposite you. The cooky plate is in the middle of each setting. The coal pile is under the table. You are not resting your head on your arms. You always look for friendly words. The victim of an assassination lies in the middle of each setting. The candelabra stand in the center of the table. A spot on a shirt is an everyday occurrence. It is not unusual for the knife to slip on the plate. Your neighbor's hand is resting on the knife. You do not swallow the wrong way. You converse to your left and to your right. (*Again the inordinately slow music has come on with a crash that is not recognizable as music at first. Houses crumble, bombs crash, but at a great distance; the text is gradually made unintelligible by the noises and finally is entirely suppressed; in between the audience begins to hear the buzzer as well as taped chimes; rattling, gongs, factory sirens as well as the theater buzzer that calls the audience back to the auditorium.*)

LX

While the lights in the auditorium are slowly dimmed in a theatrical manner, the open stage is only moderately lighted. The objects are in exactly the same position as before the intermission. The closet is open. Two Kaspars are sitting on the sofa, close together. They are silent. The masks now evince an expression of content-ment. After a few moments of silence, the prompters begin to recite all over the room:

LXI

While giving a beating
one is
never as calm as while beating a
rug.
Water dripping regularly
down on one's head
is no reason
to complain about a lack of order
a sip of acid in one's mouth
or a kick in the guts
or two sticks
in the nostrils being wriggled
about
or something on that order
only more pointed
introduced
into the ears
without much ado
to needle someone
and bring him around
with all means
at one's command
primarily
without being fussy about the
means
is no reason
to loose any words over the lack

KASPAR

of order:
for
in the process
of putting-into-order
for better or worse
one makes others sing
whereas one—
once everything has been brought
to order
and everything that still laughed
is laughable—
can sing oneself
and after giving a beating
when fists and feet have nothing
left to
do
can beat the rug to ease one's
mind.

*A third Kaspar with a small
package wrapped in wrapping
paper comes out of the wings and
sits down next to the other two
Kaspars, sits down in an orderly
fashion, the package on his knees.*

In the process of putting-into-order
one is not as calm
and orderly
as later on
when one—
having been brought into order
oneself
by the thrashing one has given to
others—
with one's conscience at ease
wants to
and can
enjoy
a world made orderly.

A fourth Kaspar comes on stage
with a similar package. Kaspar 3
makes room for him between
himself and the other two Kaspars.
Kaspar 4 sits down quietly. All
four Kaspars are still.

While giving a beating
it is sensible
not to think of the future
but in the pauses
between punches
it is blissful
to think of the time of order
so that
a too disorderly kick
won't contribute
during the recommencement of the
beating
to channel the thoughts
of the socially sick
when he has adjusted
later on
in the wrong direction.

A fifth Kaspar enters with a similar
but perhaps larger package. Kaspar
3 gets up. Kaspar 5 takes Kaspar 3's
place. Kaspar 3 squeezes himself
into the small space left next to
Kaspar 4. Kaspar 5 puts the
package in front of him on the
floor. All five are still.

But if
during the beating
an inordinate beating of the heart
fails to occur
and the fists
beat
the breath out of the victim's

KASPAR

lungs
only (to use the same image
again)
like dust
out of a rug
and one only
straightens out (to use the same
image again)
the wretch's tongue
like fringes on a rug
only then does
the injustice occur:
for
while giving a beating
one should not be as calm
as when beating a rug
while plugging up the mouth
one must be uneasy:
so as not to become uneasy
afterwards:
the failure of an inordinate
beating
of the beater's heart while
he is giving a beating
is bad:
for
anyone whose hand has trembled
suitably
while giving a beating
has a clean slate
and is one more person
who will have to have no qualms
later on:
thus calm reigns on earth.

*The original Kaspar comes on
stage as he did at first, but without
having to look for the slit in the
curtain. His movements are
self-assured and he looks like the
other Kaspars. His mask too should*

show a contented expression. He
walks with firm steps to the front
of the stage, as though to take a
bow, nicely avoiding all objects.
He stops in front of the
microphone. All six Kaspars are
still.

Those who have been brought to
order—
instead of withdrawing into
themselves
and fleeing society—
should now realistically seek
without force or beatings
but out of their own strength
to show new ways
by looking for sentences
valid for all:
they cannot choose
they must choose
and tell the others
the truth about themselves
without phrases
or bubbles:
the others too
should finally be able to want to do
what they themselves
now want and should do.

LXII
Kaspar, at the microphone, begins
to speak. His voice begins to
resemble the voices of the
prompters.
Already long
in the world
I realized nothing
I wondered
about the self-evident
and found everything finite

KASPAR

and infinite
laughable
every object filled me with fear
the whole world galled me
neither did I want to be myself
nor somebody else
my own hand
was unknown to me
my own legs
walked of their own accord
I slept
deeply
with open
eyes:
I was without consciousness
like someone drunk
and though I was supposed to be
I wanted not to be
of use
to anything
each sight
produced dislike
each sound
deceiv-
ed me
about itself
each new step
produced
nausea and sucking
in my chest
I could not keep up
I blocked my view
myself
no light
lit up for me
with the whole mishmash
of sentences
it never occurred to me
that it was I who was meant
I noticed nothing of what
was happening

around me
before I began
to come onto the world.

He is quiet for a moment or more.
The other Kaspars behind him are
also rather still.

I felt
the cacophony
the screaming
outside
was a roaring
and gurgling
in my guts:
I had to suffer,
could not distinguish
among anything:
three was not more
than two
and when I sunned myself
it rained
while I
when I was sweating
in the sun
or heating myself
running
fought my sweat with an umbrella
I could keep nothing apart
neither hot from cold
nor black from white
neither yesterday from today
nor the new from the old
neither people from things
neither prayer from cursing
neither caressing from kicking
every room
looked flat
to me
and hardly
was I awake
when the flat objects

KASPAR

fell all over me
like a dream image:
they became obstacles
all the unknown objects
interrogated me
at once
all indistinguishables confused
my hands
and made me wild
so that I became
lost
among the objects
lost my way
and
to find my way out
destroyed them.

He is quiet for a few moments.
The Kaspars behind him are quiet
too.

I came into the world
not by the clock
but because
the pain
while falling
helped me drive
a wedge
between me
and the objects
and finally extirpate
my babbling:
thus the hurt finally drove
the confusion out of me.

I learned to fill
all empty spaces with words
and learned who was who
and to pacify everything that
screamed
with sentences
no empty pot

confuses my brain box any more
everything is at my will
never
again
will I tremble
before an empty closet
before empty boxes
empty
rooms
I hesitate before no walk
out into the open
for every crack
in the wall I
have sentences
as
lists
that help me
to keep the situation
under control:

*He now raises his tone. The light
becomes brighter. The other
Kaspars are still silent.*

Everyone must be free
Everyone must be part of the scene
Everyone must know what he
wants
for the nonce
no one
may miss the drill
no one
may kill
himself in the morning
everyone must do his living
everyone must do his best
everyone must reach the rest
no one may walk across bodies
no one may stand in the lobbies
everyone must be able to spy
into everyone's eye
everyone

KASPAR

must grant
everyone
what is his.

*The other Kaspars on the sofa
begin to emit peculiar noises
whose significance is unmistakable.
The audience hears suggestions of
stylized sobbing, imitation wind
sounds, giggling.*

Everyone must be
his own man
everyone must see
to the bottom of the can
everyone must watch firmly
the other's lips
no one may blindly
trust the other's flips
everyone must see
the other's good side too
no one may willy
nilly
pooh pooh
what pleases
the other one
everyone
must let
himself be led
no one may let
lies to be spread
about anyone.

*To some extent simultaneously
with Kaspar 1's speaking, the
audience hears grumbling,
croaking, lamenting, falsetto
singing, owl-like hooting coming
from behind him.*

Everyone must work
on himself
everyone must shirk

quarreling
with his inner self
or with others
everyone must not forget to care
for others
everyone must think of the future
and share
everyone must feel
everyone must feel
secure

The audience hears rustling, leaves
slapping against each other,
ululations, roaring, laughter,
humming, purring, warbling, and
a single sharp scream.

Everyone must wash his hands
before eating
everyone must empty his pockets
before a beating
in jail
no one may dump his pail
on his own doorstep
no one may eat out of the other's
lap
everyone must care for his brother
everyone must be combed for the
meal mother
no one may let the other whimper
and wail
everyone must lend a fingernail
no one may drink coffee
from the saucer or sink
everyone must wave to his
neighbor and wink
everyone must cut his nails
before lunch
no one may make life a misery
for the other bunch
no one may soil
the clean doilies

KASPAR

everyone must clean his nose
everyone should smell like a rose
no one may make fools of others
with jokes
no one may laugh at other blokes
no one may laugh at others
no one may tickle
during the burial
no one may scribble
on toilet walls

no one may crinkle
the law books
everyone must listen to everyone
everyone must feel for everyone
everyone must tell everyone
his name.

*In the meantime, the noises and
sounds in the background have
risen to such an extent that Kaspar
in front must raise his voice more
and more. At the end of his
rhymes, the other Kaspars are still
sitting quietly on the sofa—trilling,
twittering, clearing their throats,
groaning, heckling, etc. But these
sounds have let Kaspar's speech
become so loud that the last words
resemble the thunderous ending of
a speech.*

LXIII
*The Kaspars in back are quiet for
the moment. Kaspar in front
begins to sing, perhaps falsetto.
Slowly but surely the prompters
chime in, in canon fashion, which,
however, is not resolved. They sing
softly and delicately, so that
Kaspar is intelligible throughout.
Kaspar sings like a true believer.*

No one may bite the fork
with his teeth
no one may mention
murderers
at dinner
no one may transport private

persons
in the official car
everyone must be worth everyone's
while
no one may call a man by another
man's
name
no one may live unregistered
everyone should buy heavy goods
only on the way home
no one may ridicule anyone just
because
he has thick lips
no one may tap anyone on
the shoulder
no one may stick
a knife
between anyone's
ribs
everyone must call a cop
on the street
officer sir

*The Kaspars in back also sing
along, but not words, only sounds.
Nor do they really sing. They
screech, yodel, buzz, trumpet,
draw snot into their noses, smack
their lips, grunt, burp, ululate,
etc.: all of it in rhythm with the
song. Now they grow gradually
louder.*

None of the furniture may
catch dust
no hungry man may
stand in line and rest
no adolescent may
loiter
no beanpole may reach the height
of the high-
voltage wires

KASPAR

no flag may flutter
like a goiter
in the wrong direction
all morality must
come into being
I trust
during work
every animal that remains what it is
must yield
to the animal that sheds its skin
on the field
every word that does not mean
well
must be cut.

*The Kaspars in back become
louder still. One of them unwraps
his package, the paper rustling
loudly in the process, takes a nail
file from the package and begins
filing his nails. Another Kaspar
repeats the process, rustling the
paper even more loudly and taking
an even bigger file out of his
package to file his nails with.
Filing noises can already be heard.*

No elbow on the table
no fish with the knife
no parasite
with the fingers
no spoon
with its side to the mouth
no solace
for tired eyes
no truffles uncooked
every bum in jail:
kill every paradox

Kaspar 1 is speaking again:

No shit on a real stick

*The prompters sing what Kaspar
utters, and the other Kaspars
squeak, bark, make the sounds of*

no genuine finger for lick-
ing
every fresh fish for fry-
ing
every true person
in the clear about every-
thing
every truly healthy fruit
fling
in the can
everything unessential
down the drain

*rain and storm, blow up bubble
gum till it bursts, etc.*

LXIV
*He stops speaking. There is
silence. Then Kaspar says:*

What was it
that
I said
just now?
If I only knew
what it is
that I said
just now!
If I only knew
what I said
just now!
What is that
that I said
just now?
What
was I
actually
saying
just now?
What was it
that was
being said
just now?

KASPAR

If I only knew
what I
said
just now!
What
was that
actually
that I was
saying
just now?

Even while he is asking himself these questions, he, like the other Kaspars, begins to giggle and the like. At the same time the prompters sing his previous verses to the end. Kaspar, for instance, is snapping his finger against the microphone, producing a whine. All the Kaspars, while the prompters are singing, finally emit genuinely infectious laughter. Finally, sighing and giggling, the speaking Kaspar and the other Kaspars gradually grow quiet. The audience hears two or three of them filing their nails.
Kaspar in front says:
Every sentence
is for the birds
every sentence is for
the birds
every sentence is for the birds
There is silence.
He begins to speak without versifying.
A spotlight is on him.
I was proud of the first step I took, of the second step I felt ashamed; I was just as proud of the first hand which I discovered on myself, but of the second hand I felt ashamed: I felt ashamed of everything that I repeated; yet I felt ashamed even of the first sentence I uttered, whereas I no longer felt ashamed of the second sentence and soon became accustomed to the subsequent ones. I was proud of my second sentence.

In my story I only wanted to make a noise with my first sentence, whereas with my second sentence I wanted to call attention to myself, and I wanted to *speak* with the next sentence, and I wanted to *hear* myself *speak* with the next sentence, and with my next sentence I wanted *others* to hear my speaking, and with the next sentence I wanted others to hear *what* I said, and with the next sentence I wanted others who *also* uttered a sentence not to be heard, and used only the next to last sentence to *ask questions*, and began only with the last sentence of the story to ask what the *others* had said, the others who were ignored while I said my sentence.

I saw the snow and attacked the snow. Thereupon I said the sentence: I want to be a person like somebody else was once, with which I wanted to express why the snow was biting my hands. Once I woke up in the dark and saw nothing. Thereupon I said: I want to be a person like somebody else was once, with which I wanted to express, first of all, why is it that the whole room has been moved away, and then, because I did not see myself, why have I been cut off from everything that belongs to me, whereupon, because I had heard someone, namely myself, speaking, I said once more: I want to be a person like somebody else was once?—with which I wanted to express that I would have liked to have known who else was making fun of me while I was speaking. Then once I took a look into the open, where there was a very green glow, and I said to the open: I want to be a person like somebody else was once?—and with this sentence I wanted to ask the open why it was that my feet were aching. I also noticed a curtain that was moving. Thereupon I said, but not to the curtain: I want to be a person like somebody else was once, and with that I wanted to say, but not to the curtain, I don't know to whom, why are all the table drawers out and why does my coat always get caught in the door. I also heard someone climbing stairs which creaked, and thereupon I said to the creaking that I want to be a person like somebody else was once, with which I wanted to express when will my head feel lighter again. Once I also let my plate fall to the floor, but it did not break, whereupon I exclaimed: I want to be a person like somebody else was once, with which I meant that I was afraid of nothing in the world, whereupon I said once more: I want to be a person like somebody else was once, with which I wanted to make comprehensible that something probably could make me afraid, for example a cracked icicle; and once I felt no more pain, and I shouted: I want to be a person like somebody else was once, with which I wanted to say to everyone that I finally felt no more pain, but then I felt pain once more and I whispered in everyone's ear: I want to be a person like somebody else was once, with which I wanted to inform everyone that no, on the contrary, I felt no more pain and that everything was all right with me, with which I began to lie; and finally I said to myself: I want to be a person like somebody else was once, and wanted to know with that what that sentence, which I said to myself, what it actually means.

Because the snow was white and because snow was the first white I saw, I called everything white snow. I was given a handkerchief that was white, but I believed it would bite me because the white snow bit my hand when I touched it, and I did not touch the handkerchief, and when I knew the word snow I called the white handkerchief snow: but later, when I also knew the word handkerchief, when I saw a white handkerchief, even when I uttered the word handkerchief, I still thought the word snow, because of which I first began to remember. But a brown or gray handkerchief was not snow, just as the first brown or gray snow I saw was not snow, but the first gray or brown that I saw, for example animal droppings or a sweater. But a white wall was snow, and just as much as absolutely everything became snow when I looked into the sun for a long time, because I then saw only snow. Finally I even used the word snow, out of curiosity, for something that was not white, to see whether it would turn to snow because of my uttering the word snow, and even if I did not say the word snow I was thinking it and remembered at every sight if not the snow itself at least the word snow. Even while falling asleep or while walking along a country lane or while running in the dark I kept saying the word snow all the time. But finally I reached the point where I no longer believed not only words and sentences about snow, but even the snow itself when it lay there in front of me or was falling, did not believe any more and held it neither for real nor as possible, only because I no longer believed the word snow.

The landscape at that time was a brightly colored window shutter. As of the time that I saw the shadow a chair cast on the floor, I have from that time on always designated a fallen chair on the floor as the shadow of a chair. Each movement was running because at that time I wanted to do nothing but run and run away from everything; even swimming in the water was running. Jumping was running in the wrong direction. Even falling was running. Every liquid, even when it was calm, was a possible running. When I was afraid, the objects ran very quickly. But nightfall at that time was becoming unconscious.

When I did not know where to turn next, it was explained to me that I was afraid when I did not know where to turn, and that is how I learned to be afraid; and when I saw red it was explained to me that I was angry; but when I wanted to crawl away to hide I was ashamed; and when I leapt into the air I was happy; but when I was near bursting I had a secret or was proud of something; and when I nearly expired I had pity; but when I knew neither left nor right I was in despair; and when I did not know what was up or down I was confused; but when my breath stopped I was startled; and when I became ashen-faced I was afraid of death; but when I rubbed my hands together I was satisfied; and when I stuttered it was explained to me that I was happy when I stuttered; when I stuttered I was happy.

After I had learned to say the word I, I had to be addressed as I for

KASPAR

a time because I did not know I was meant by the word you, since I was called I; and also, when I already knew the word you I pretended for a time that I did not know who was meant, because I enjoyed not understanding anything; thus I also began to enjoy responding whenever the word you was uttered.

When I did not understand a word I doubled it and doubled it once more, so that it would no longer bother me. I said: war, war; rag, rag. I said: war, war, war, war; rag, rag, rag, rag. Thus I became accustomed to words.

I first saw only one person. Later, after I had seen this one person, I saw several other persons. That certainly surprised me.

I saw something sparkle. Because it sparkled, I wanted to have it. I wanted to have everything that sparkled. Later I also wanted to have what didn't sparkle.

I saw that someone had something. I wanted to have something like it. Later I also wanted to have something.

When I woke up I ate. Then I played and also spoke until I fell asleep again and woke up again.

Once I put my hands in my pockets and could not pull them out again.

Once every object seemed to me to prove something, but what?

Once (*he tries to swallow*) I was unable to swallow.

Meantime, one of the Kaspars has taken a large file out of his carton and rasped once across the carton. Thereupon he also begins to file on the Kaspar sitting next to him. The sound produced by the filing is of the kind that drives one wild. All the Kaspars wear some kind of material which, if a file, knife, or nail is applied to it, produces all manner of excruciating noises. Up to this point, only one of these noises has been produced, and briefly. The Kaspars might have on their clothing pieces of foam rubber, tin, stone, slate, etc. All these are in the carton. One might also use the noise produced by crumpling the wrapping paper. The noises now become increasingly more frequent and louder because all the Kaspars in back begin to work on the cartons and on each other with their files, knives, slate pencils, nails, fingernails, etc. One by one, they get up and form a tight, wrangling huddle. However, each noise is distinct from the others: none is produced indiscriminately; nor do they drown out the words of Kaspar 1 at the microphone; on the contrary, they make them even more distinct.

Once (*he tries to sneeze*) I was
unable to sneeze.

Once (*he tries to yawn*) I was
unable to yawn.

Once—(*with effort he tries to
speak the following sentence to
the end*) pursue the others . . . I
caught . . . no one vanquished
. . . the objects were . . . I drove
. . . no one caressed . . . the
others stormed . . . the objects
had . . . no one pushed . . . I
shoved . . . the others showed
. . . the objects became . . . I
moved . . . the others ripped
. . . no one lowered . . . the
objects are . . . the objects have
. . . the others rub . . . no one
hits . . . I drag . . . the objects
become . . . no one chokes . . .
the others get . . . —I was unable
to speak a sentence to the end.

Once made slip slip . . . once
madip slip slip . . . once madip
slin slin . . . monce mamin
m:m:m . . . —I made a slip of
the tongue, and they all looked at
each other.

Once I was the only one who
laughed.

Once I sat down on a fly.

Once I heard everyone scream
murder! but when I looked I only
found a peeled tomato in the
garbage can.

All at once I distinguished myself
from the furnishings.

Already with my first sentence I
was trapped.

*The sounds become increasingly
more ample and prolonged. For
instance, one will hear the sound
of a door scraping along a stone
floor, of a metal bar slipping along
a polar bear's claws in a circus, of
a sled running its runners from
snow onto gravel, of chalk or a
fingernail on slate, of a knife
scraping a plate, of people scraping
a marble floor with nails in their
shoes, of a saw cutting through
new wood, of a fingernail scraping
across a pane of glass, of cloth
tearing, etc. (Leave something to
the imagination, but not too
much.) As these noises are
produced, and as the various
objects in the cartons (foam
rubber, etc.) are cut up, the
Kaspars gradually come to the
front of the stage.*

KASPAR

I can make myself understood. I think I must have slept a long time because I am awake now. I go to the table and use the table, but look at that—the table continues to exist after it has been used. I can appear because I know where my place is. I cannot fall asleep with dry hands, but when I spit into my hands they become even drier. By saying: the chair is harmless, it is all over with the chair's harmlessness. I feel good when the door, having stood open for long, is finally closed. I know where everything belongs. I have a good eye for the right proportion. I don't put anything into my mouth. I can laugh to three. I am usable. I can hear wood rotting over long distances. I no longer understand anything literally. I cannot wait until I wake up, whereas earlier I could not wait to fall asleep. I have been made to speak. I have been converted to reality. —Do you hear it? (*Silence.*) Can you hear? (*Silence.*) Psst. (*Silence.*)

The stage becomes dark.
Silence.

LXV
As the stage becomes bright once more, the events on stage are again divided into three parts: together with Kaspar's speech as follows, the prompters come on again. Whispering, they repeat something like this: If only. Own future. Now every second one as opposed to every fourth one at one time. A possible object. If only. Make life easier. If only. Development. If only. In reality. If only. In constantly growing numbers. If only. Serves the. If only. Bears dangers. If only. It is necessary for that. If only. *Finally, they repeat over and over again, until the end, speaking softly:* If only. If only. If only. *Meanwhile, the Kaspars come forward (filing, etc.) and proceed to manhandle the speaking Kaspar with their files, etc. They make particular fun of one object, say a chair, laughing at it, imitating it, costuming it, dragging it off and imitating the sound it makes as it is being dragged across the floor, thus making it utterly ridiculous*

and making it and all other objects COMPLETELY IMPOSSIBLE. *Kaspar 1 has gone on speaking:*

I can hear the logs comfortably crackling in the fire, with which I want to say that I do not hear the bones crackling comfortably. The chair stands here, the table there, with which I mean to say that I am telling a story. I would not like to be older, but I would like for much time to have passed, with which I mean to say that a sentence is a monster, with which I mean to say that speaking can help temporarily, with which I mean to say that every object becomes ticklish when I am startled. I say: I can imagine to be everywhere now, except that I cannot imagine really being there, with which I mean to say that the doorknobs are empty. I can say: the air snaps shut, or: the room creaks, or: the curtain jingles, with which I mean to say that I don't know where I should put or leave my hand, while I when I say that I don't know where to put my hand mean to say that all doors tempt me only under the pretense that they can be opened, which sentence I would like to use in the sense of: my hair has gotten into the table as into a machine and I am scalped: literally: with each new sentence I become nauseous: figuratively: I have been turned topsy-turvy: I am in someone's hand: I look to the other side: there prevails an unbloody calm: I cannot rid myself of myself any more: I toss the hat onto the meathook: every stool helps while dying: the furnishings are waterproof: the furniture is as it ought to be: nothing is open: the pain and its end come within sight: time must stop: thoughts become very small: I still experienced myself: I never saw myself: I put up no undue resistance: the shoes fit like gloves: I don't get away with just a fright: the skin peels off: the foot sleeps itself dead: candles and bloodsuckers: ice and mosquitoes: horses and puss: hoarfrost and rats: eels and sicklebills:

Meantime, the other Kaspars are producing an infernal noise with their various tools which they have applied to the objects they have brought with them and to Kaspar 1. They are giggling, behave

KASPAR

like crowds in crowd scenes in plays, ridicule Kaspar 1 by speaking in the same rhythm as he, etc. Kaspar 1 had also produced a file and makes similar noises by scraping with the file against the microphone while he is speaking his sentences. But now, all at once, an almost complete silence sets in. The Kaspars merely flap their arms about a little and gesticulate. They wriggle a little. They snuffle. Then Kaspar says:

Goats and monkeys

With that, the curtain jolts a little toward the center, where the Kaspars are wriggling. The jolt produces a shrill sound.

Goats and monkeys

With an even shriller sound, the curtain jerks a little farther toward the middle.

Goats and monkeys

With an even shriller sound, the curtain jerks still farther toward the middle.

Goats and monkeys

With an even shriller sound, the curtain moves still more toward the center.

Goats and monkeys

With the shrillest possible sound, the curtain makes one final jerk toward the center, where the Kaspars are still wriggling a little. The curtain slams into them the moment Kaspar 1 says his last word: it topples all of them. They fall over, but fall behind the curtain, which has now come together. The piece is over.

LaVergne, TN USA
21 July 2010
190229LV00003B/18/A